I Can Do This Thing
Called Life: and So Can You

I Can Do This Thing Called Life: and So Can You

By Cath DePalma

Wise Woman Press

I Can Do This Thing Called Life: and So Can You

By Cath DePalma

© Cath DePalma

Managing Editor: Michael Terranova

ISBN: 978-0945385-33-2

WiseWoman Press
Portland, OR 97217

www.wisewomanpress.com

Dedication

I dedicate this book to my husband, John Anthony DePalma. Without him, *I Can Do This Thing Called Life: and So Can You,* would not have been possible. John's huge heart, big vision, and inspiration are catalysts for my own ongoing growth. He is a strong presence in my life, and I am eternally grateful for him, and all of his love and support. He shows up every day ready to begin anew, no matter what. Everyone should have such a person in their life.

And to my teacher and mentor whose voice continues to speak in my head, Dr. Kennedy Shultz. He saved my life. He helped me birth a transformation in me. He taught me how to think clearly, see that I did have choices, believe that there was another way, another whole world I could have access to, know that my dreams could come true, and that I could create another life for myself with the help of the Infinite. My new life would come together by divine design. I had the pleasure of knowing him for 17 years before he made his transition. During that time, he married John and I, installed me as a new minister, performed a welcoming ceremony for Joseph, our son, when he was born, and performed my ordination.

Contents

Dedication.. v

Contents vii

Foreword.. ix

Preface xiii

Introduction.. xvii

Part 1 Spiritual Living...................................... *1*

1 Journey Into Me.. 3

2 A World That Works for All 17

3 Journey Into You.. 31

Part 2 I Can Do This *41*

4 I Can Do This Thing Called Health 43

5 I Can Do This Thing Called Love 63

6 I Can Do This Thing Called Work 87

7 I Can Do This Thing Called Wealth................. 109

8 I Can Do This Thing Called Death 127

9 The Great "AH HA" 147

10 You Are Created for Greatness........................ 151

Part 3 Spiritual Practices *155*

11 Everything's A Practice 157

12 Mind Treatment.. 171

13 Building Your Spiritual Portfolio (More tools).... 179

Part 4 Where Do We Go From Here?............... *183*

14 It's All Here.. 185

15 Love Yourself Anyway 187

16 Smooth Sailing 191

ADDENDUM **195**

IDEAL DAY 196

MIND TREATMENT 198

SACRED COVENANT 200

SACRED SPACE COVENANT 202

My Favorite Movies 203

My Favorite Books 205

Acknowledgements 207

About the Author 209

Foreword

I was not completely aware of how bad my frame of mind and thoughts had gotten, but by my mid 20's, I knew that my life was far off track from where I wanted it to be. While my attitude toward my life and future had once been happy and optimistic, it had somehow taken a turn for the worse. I had subtly become bitter, and the compassion that I had once possessed towards people was hard to find. Was peace and wholeness even possible? At what point in our lives do we become conscious enough to know that we have made some poor choices and we are responsible for the quality of our lives and relationships? That it is entirely our decision whether or not we choose fear and anger or love and peace to demonstrate on a daily basis? For myself, it was this time in my life that I discovered the secret. This was the year that I received my first blue print and instruction manual for life and living well.

Working for a large company in Atlanta, Georgia, Cath DePalma sat in the cubicle in front of me. She was not yet a reverend, but I can tell you that she had already become a teacher of life, love, and peace. At this time of my life I had many questions for God, and religion had left me with little faith. I looked with some skepticism at all the positive affirmations surrounding Cath's cubicle concerning good health, abounding prosperity, and living well. This may have been a dark time in my life, but I was searching to see if hope really existed and if there was a way to fix things. I really did want to know God, have better health, the ability to pay my bills, and most of all I wanted love. Many of my friends had already married and were starting to have children. I remember that I had just read an article in *Cosmopolitan Magazine* that reported that if you had not married by the time you were 30, then the future looked grim for you in the love department. I watched Cath in fascination as she refused to walk around, depressed and passionless about her life. She certainly had ongoing situations in her life that could have made her want to give up and join the complainers. It was at this time that I realized that it is much easier to stay a complainer, not be totally conscious, and not live life to the fullest. If life was to change for me I needed to know how to do this. I was a "prove it to me" person so I watched as Cath changed her situations and relationships by making declarations with God. As our friendship grew, she gave me information little by little, probably so as to not scare me off. Assignments that I could handle easily came my way. She would say to me, "pick something small and start affirming its existence and while you are at it, do something nice for someone even if you don't feel like it." I was learning to let go of being a victim, calling forth what I wanted, and planting sacred seeds with God as my partner.

Thanking God for all that I had already been blessed with was also important. The manifestations started rolling in and my anger and bitterness over how my life had been going was pushed out of the way enough to let faith start to grow. When faith and thankfulness start to grow in your spirit, you are never the same. My health did get better, prosperity abounded, and I met my great love and husband of now 16 years.

Many years have passed since Cath and I became friends and family. She is now a reverend and lover of God. What she taught me is now her everyday life. I will forever give thanks to my Creator for introducing me to this humble soul who was a gateway for me to know how to live life and to have a relationship with the One Power. This taught me what to do when I get myself in a mess, and how to love when it's the last thing I want to do. As you will read, Cath has given a blue print of how God and you can live this new life not plagued by fear, anger, and the ever-present attitudes of the world but filled with love, joy and what is good in this world. She embraces God as an omnipresent partner who wants nothing more than smooth sailing for our lives and to love us in this great gift called Life.

By Carol Goodman

Close friend and fellow traveler

Books are the legacies that a great genius leaves to mankind, which are delivered down from generation to generation as presents to the posterity of those who are yet unborn.

Joseph Addison 1672-1719

Preface

Shortly after becoming a minister, I led a metaphysical discussion group at Barnes and Noble bookstore for a while to spur the growth of our own spiritual community. I met wonderful people there, and some are still in my life today. One in particular, who is no longer with us, still holds a very special place in my heart. Her name was Ray. Her son, Eric, brought her to the group and from then on she started coming every Sunday morning.

One Sunday, Ray approached me and said, "You need help. I'll tell you what: You do what you do best--teach, lead, talk--and I will take care of the rest, the business part of things." I didn't know what to say. I was awestruck. There was no question that I needed help. Building a spiritual community is no easy venture. I gladly accepted Ray's offer.

We developed a very close relationship that went beyond our work together. She became a very dear friend, so close that she was the first call we made the morning of our son's birth. We were inseparable with our plans and business. We enjoyed our relationship together for six years. Because we worked so closely and shared so much, I was prepared now to go to another level in my partnership with God. I knew how it felt to be loved and supported.

At the end of our time together, Ray had completed her classwork, and was installed as an assistant minister for our center. A year later, she made her transition. She had many health problems all of her life, which she believed started in her teens when she was vaccinated. Having survived on steroids for much of her adult life, her body finally gave way, and it was a big loss to me and our community. Ray earned her "Rev." title long before she ever got it. I am forever grateful for our time together.

The time I spent with Ray was a perfect segue to me building a real, solid, everlasting partnership with God. Her death further emphasized what I had been avoiding: the need to go inside and develop my connection with Spirit. I believe there are others who are ready to experience more of themselves as well. My first reason for writing this book is to help them along the way.

My second reason for writing this book is to explore the deeper meaning of 9/11. There are days in our lives that we will never forget, and for me, that fateful Tuesday morning is one of them. It is comparable to the day, as a 4th grader in P.E. class, when President John F. Kennedy was assassinated.

It didn't take long for me to realize that I had been preparing for 9/11 my whole life, especially when I began my spiritual quest and study in the mid-eighties. This investment in my spirituality paid off generously by giving me a greater peace of mind, freeing me up to more love, and helping me to forgive myself. It was the impetus for getting to know myself in a greater way. I was able to see from a healthier, more loving perspective, realize how much I am a part of Life, and how loved and supported I was. This spirituality not only made a huge impact in my own life, but it made a huge difference in the life of my family and all the other lives I touched and continues to be a rich resource for me to draw upon.

Somehow I always knew we were all being prepared for a bigger picture. I never imagined it would come as quickly and violently as it did that day. One minute everything was business as usual, and the next our twin towers were demolished, whole groups of people were gone, and both our nation and the world were in shock from all that transpired.

How do we face tragedy in our lives and the world? What moves us through it and beyond? Spiritual transformation hardly appears like we think it should. It doesn't even necessarily feel good. Extreme situations do bring out the very best and open us up to greater love. On a larger scale, 9/11 allowed us to take a look, globally in fact, at ourselves and our beliefs, what we valued, who we were. We got to see our vulnerabilities and our strengths and how essential it is for us to have a more spiritual foundation from which to work.

9/11 has brought us to a culminating point, an era in the evolution of human consciousness where we have to make a decision. Are we victims to groups of people, weather patterns, or the economy, or are we powerful creators who continuously create our world with our thoughts? If we are creators, what part do we play in the collective consciousness which creates the reality we are all living?

We don't always know what we are here to do. There are things we put off because we are afraid of what it will mean to be more of ourselves and the changes that will come along with it. Stepping into a bigger picture of ourselves is no easy task. As we open ourselves up to our spiritual nature and align ourselves with Life, we get a more expansive perspective, come from a greater love and live from that fuller, richer place within ourselves that is infinite. We have everything within us to do just that.

There really is much more to us than meets the eye. We are always being called within ourselves and Life to a depth that we have barely touched.

My third reason for writing is that I have always been fascinated with books. You could say that I have always been a book worm. I knew in my early twenties that one day I would write a book. I sat down at that time, ready to write, and nothing came out. I didn't have enough experience. I hadn't lived yet. Add another 30 years and there's quite a tale.

Returning to my real self has been the greatest gift I have given myself. Now, I pass this on. I invite you, my sisters and brothers everywhere throughout the planet, to go inside and experience the preciousness, the beauty, and the wonder of your own innermost being. This book is my gift back to the world for all I have been given along the way. Emma Curtis Hopkins, mystic and metaphysical teacher of the early 1900's put it this way:

In this world each of us has all we can do to look to the ways of our own heart, ensuring that our thoughts and world are in harmony by thinking as our heart is thinking, instead of from any imagination of sin or mistake.

Introduction

This book is a story about me, and just as importantly, about you. It's about all of us, being as we are, human beings. Just ask yourself some questions:

What about you? What's your story? Ever feel as though you are in deep, over your head, involved in something--a relationship, problem, particular line of work, or an unhealthy pattern with no apparent way out?

Ever feel as though you are going down a road that you just don't want to be going down, that you took the wrong turn, made a decision that has you going in a whole, different direction and every step of the way seems wrong? Does it seem that there's no turning back.

Ever find yourself waiting for something that appears to be out of reach? Something that affects you that is really happening to someone close to you or to the people you work with? Are you waiting for something outside of yourself to change so that you can be free of it, complete with it?

Ever wanted something to happen that just never does?

Are you tired of bringing forth time, energy and money with no apparent benefit?

At one point or another I have said "yes" to all these questions. Maybe you have said "yes" to some of them too. But there is always another way to look at things. There are different ways of doing things that can create more happiness and fulfillment for us. Whatever you think is in your way is merely a distraction that keeps you from being all that you were meant to be.

My story of evolving consciousness started in my mid 30's. It was the late '80's and for the first time since college I was living alone in Atlanta. My mother came to visit me there. There had been a tension between us since I had left the Catholic Church. For years I was a "nothing," and now I had found this strange New Thought teaching, Science of Mind. We sat down the first night of her visit after dinner and I said, "Mom, you know we want the same thing. We are talking about the same God and we really both want good for everyone."

I will never forget that night. From then on there was a peace between us that wasn't there before. We went beyond trying to persuade, defend, or accuse each other concerning our spiritual beliefs. We moved to the field beyond the boundaries of our religious beliefs to common ground. It seemed that we had became spiritual equals. Interestingly, she prayed all her life to have a priest in the family. So far, all she had was a minister daughter. Life doesn't always go the way we imagine yet everything seems to fit into place.

Whether we call it Buddha, Allah, Spirit, Life, God, Energy, Infinite Mind, Intelligence, Source, Love, Good, or anything I have not included, we are really talking about the same Entity. IT is the same Power and Presence that works with us all. There is only One, and we are all really living the One Life of Spirit together. How can anyone's idea of God be better than another's when it is the very same God we are talking about? Is it possible for any of us to describe and understand an infinite God? Hardly, and yet, there is no reason why we shouldn't try because there is much we can learn.

In this book, we will honor IT, *The Thing ITself*, a phrase coined by Ernest Holmes in an attempt to eliminate the inherent gender aspect given to the traditional western God, the Ultimate Stuff out of which all Life is made, the One, God, or Source of us all by varying the name. Whatever name puts you in touch with the divine is most meaningful for you to use. It is all the same thing and so there is no right or wrong name. We honor and respect whatever name you choose.

All Roads Lead Home. We each have our own path. While we share this life experience together, our own experience is unique and we each have a singular perspective in the whole universe. There are no two things exactly alike, not a grain of sand or blade of grass. An infinite creator never makes copies of the same thing, person or situation. IT is fully capable of coming up with a new and different creation every time. Even if we share the exact same philosophy of Life, the road traveled will be different for each one of us. We have our own ideal path which is perfect for us. I share my path with you only as a guide or to give you a glimpse of what is possible for your own. There is a flame within you that is eternally guiding and directing you. When you follow it, you can't help but be happy.

We are infinite beings and so this beautiful unfoldment goes on for eternity. We are forever getting to know ourselves more deeply. There is no final destination. There is completion with certain segments of life and even then, our thoughts and ideas continue to grow. As we review what has already transpired in our lives, we have a chance to see how much we have grown. I have declared this book finished even though my thoughts evolve and expand with each minute, giving me a greater wisdom and perspective. In reality, the book is never complete. I have given you my very best even though it may be different tomorrow as I continue to change.

You Are Exactly Where You Need To Be. What I discuss in this book may seem unbelievable to some. Some may say that it can't be proven. I know the mental work behind the scenes that goes into the creation of my demonstrations or results. As far as I am concerned and the reason I continue is because I totally believe what I have manifested is quantifiable. You will have to work with this way of thinking on your own. The study of Life really is meaningless until you can prove how it really works in your life. Where do you begin? You can begin anywhere. You just have to start. Life, on the physical level, is a big experiment. We are here to play, test it, and learn how to work with IT.

Some of this may seem overwhelming to those who are new to this way of thinking. There is no rush to arrive at where you think you need to be or even want to be. No one else has the power to insist that you be a certain way or be at a particular place in consciousness. A great deal of love, kindness, and compassion are needed as we all find our way. Sooner or later we will move ahead because life is set up for us to win. You are at the right place along your perfect path. You have been all along. Pay attention to what is calling you, and drawing you towards it. If there is energy there, it may be the next step. Do what feels right to your heart and trust your instincts. You are getting exactly what you need right where you are.

I Can Do This and So Can You! We spend a lot of time trying to convince ourselves that we can't do life, that it's too hard, that we can't possibly understand God or Life, that we aren't good enough, we are flawed, and we could never do such and such. We have our reasons as to why our lives aren't what they could be, or a story about what has defeated us, and why things will never be the same. We find others who will sympathize with us and relate their own version of life's obstacle course. Has any of that talk ever gotten you anywhere? Certainly, it has never gotten me anywhere.

What if we believed we could do something about our lives, our feelings, our thoughts, and the situations we find ourselves in? We want to believe that it is possible for us to succeed, and that our life matters. What we don't know is that *We CAN Do This Thing Called Life* and are already doing it. We are already a success by just being here.

The beginning chapters talk about the journey into ourselves where we face our fears and ultimately get to know who we really are. Next we take a look at spiritual living and how to create a world that works for all. How can we see ourselves in a new light from that bigger perspective?

In Part 2, *I Can Do This*, we will address specific areas of your life: health, wealth, creative expression or work, love, and death. These are the cornerstones to a strong, spiritual foundation.

We begin with, *I Can Do This Thing Called Health*. What is behind our health? Why are some people healthy and others are not? Do you believe you are stuck with your current conditions or that health deteriorates as you age? Decide to be healthy and learn how to stay young, energetic and alive your whole life.

I Can Do This Thing Called Love. What is behind our love? Why are some people enjoying more love in their lives while others are not? Do you believe you are doomed to a life without love or stuck with unhealthy relationships forever? Learn how to get into a loving relationship with yourself. Then attract healthy, loving, supportive relationships. Life was never meant to be lonely.

I Can Do This Thing Called Creative Expression or Work. What is behind our work? Why do some people have the best jobs while others get the boring, meaningless ones? Is it your lot in life to stay where you are forever or is there something more for you in the area of self-expression or work? Take a look into a greater possibility for yourself starting now.

I Can Do This Thing Called Wealth. What is behind our wealth? Are you trapped in your current financial state for life? Were you created to barely survive or is there more? Learn how to look past your current situation and find a way to create more wealth in your life.

I Can Do This Thing Called Death. What is death really? Is it something to dread or is it a natural part of life? Working closely with death as a minister, I was surprised to see how much different it was from what the world believes. There is much more to transitioning from this life. I have included this chapter because I believe if we can see death for what it really is, we will rid ourselves of so much dread and fear. Make friends with the so-called "enemy" and see how free your life becomes.

Part 3 is full of *Spiritual Practices*. To help support you in your life, we will discuss different spiritual practices and provide you with tools that you can use regularly to engage in a deeper, more satisfying relationship with yourself and Life.

Throughout the work, you will notice that I use the word, *treatment* or the phrases, *mind treatment*, or *prayer treatment*. They are synonymous terms referring to a form of affirmative prayer. Affirmative prayer claims that we already have our desire. We believe we have our good before we actually see it. It's not the typical way we look at prayer. Typically, we are told to pray and left alone to figure out what to do. We may memorize some traditional prayers that we can then recite. Traditionally, we are asking God for help with something. Treatment is not begging, beseeching or even bargaining with God. It aligns us with our Source making it possible to see what is already here for us.

Mind treatment is a step-by-step tool for shifting consciousness, moving our minds in a more specific way. Usually, we react to something someone is saying, to something happening in our world, to health conditions, or to something going on with our families. Most of our thoughts have to do with our past choices and our fears about the future. Mind treatment takes us beyond this commonplace thinking and puts us in touch with a spiritual perspective.

Mind Treatment was created by Ernest Holmes as a form of praying that realigns our minds with the Universal Mind: the One Mind or Truth. I will be talking more specifically about this concept later in the book, but for now, whenever I use words relating to treatment, this is the process I am referring to.

Lastly in Part 4 *Where Do We Go From Here?* you are invited to see an expanded view of yourself. It was the famous Walt Whitman who said, "You are not all included between your hat and your boots." Stepping out of the world as you know it into a new one takes courage. Get into a whole new picture of how Life works and how you can work with IT. See that we live in an intelligent universe that knows exactly what IT is doing, and how perfectly IT is already working for us all.

Even though it is important to intellectually understand the science behind living successfully, it is more important for us to learn how to put it into practice. If we are to see consistent, successful results or demonstrations from our mind treatments, we have to prove how this principle works in our lives. Once we prove the principle with hard evidence, we can expand on it and duplicate it over and over again. As we do this, we evolve and thereby creating more greatly as we go.

Now, know this: You Are the "One". You may not know this, but you have been preparing for this time. You are the "One" you have been waiting for. If you feel you are not ready, it is not too late to become more prepared. Now, more than ever, is the time to embark on a journey that will take you places you never dreamed possible: one that will help you create a new life for yourself. If everyone does this for themselves, we will create a more beautiful world for us all.

It's time to get in touch and become one with that infinite center of Life within you, that unshakeable core at the center of your being. It's time to invest in activities that feed and nourish your soul and make you strong. We must be sustainable from within before we can be sustainable from without. That is why you are here. There is no accident to you being alive at this time. Some part of you has asked for more out of life. All that Infinite Intelligence, God or Source has to offer is already here for you. Maybe it's time to stop resisting and blocking your good. Say yes, fully prepared to let go of limiting beliefs in order to gain infinite life. You are more than enough to take this on. You can do this. We all can.

It is time to release and let go of everything that we have outgrown or that no longer serves us. It is time for us to make space for the new and be open to receive all the good that is already here for us.

It's time to build our life, our home, our world on a spiritually sound foundation that is stable and give up the life we have created on shifting sands. That old life is tired and will never get us where we want to go or give us what we truly desire: more God.

I know in every fiber of my being, you can overcome whatever challenge or difficulty you may be experiencing and step into a greater idea of yourself and a greater possibility for your life. The Universe in all of IT's magnificence and glory, loves and supports you right where you are.

Your very own journey awaits you. Are you ready?

You Are "The Power" of your life. You Can Do This Thing Called Life!

Let's take the first steps together.

Part 1
Spiritual Living

1
Journey Into Me

The Road Not Taken

Two roads diverged in a yellow wood,
And sorry I could not travel both
And be one traveler, long I stood
And looked down one as far as I could
To where it bent in the undergrowth;
Then took the other, as just as fair,
And having perhaps the better claim,
Because it was grassy and wanted wear;
Though as for that the passing there
Had worn them really about the same,
And both that morning equally lay
In leaves no step had trodden black.
Oh, I kept the first for another day!
Yet knowing how way leads on to way,
I doubted if I should ever come back.
I shall be telling this with a sigh
Somewhere ages and ages hence:
Two roads diverged in a wood, and I –
I took the one less traveled by,
And that has made all the difference.

Robert Frost

As I prepare the final chapters of this book, I find I need a getaway…some solitude, some place where I can hear myself think. I have been getting a call to isolate myself and *be*. It doesn't matter how wonderful your everyday life is, you still need to get away from it every now and then and take care of yourself. I have a wonderful marriage of seventeen years with my husband, John. We have three beautiful children; Nick and Liz are grown and Joseph just turned 12. Our youngest son is colorful, interesting, beautiful, and a joy to have around. He also demands a lot of attention that we are happy to give because we know how important the time is that we have together. Although we fall into the category of older parents, Joseph keeps us hopping and filled with youthfulness.

John and I are spiritual directors for a community we took over 17 years ago. We work with people who are serious about their spirituality and ready to step into a bigger picture of themselves and their lives; specifically, they are prepared to move toward spiritual maturity, tap into their divine potential, and live from a more loving place. Through our work with others, we grow as well. Though there is no standing still and work is never ending, John and I love our calling. While it is difficult to get away, taking time away to ourselves is essential to our work and our life.

I have been using every excuse there is to distract myself from doing what I am being called to do, which is to finish this book: my mother's transition two years ago, the remodeling of our kitchen and bathroom last year, our family, our work, the holidays, and so on. There is always something going on, focus is needed. Courage is also necessary. Working on the book is growing and stretching me even more.

In November, I tell Sam, my close friend and mind treatment partner, that I really need to get away to work on my book. It is so great to have a personal coach and friend, someone to bounce ideas off of, who knows me and loves me no matter what. I love the work we do together. It has become a very large part of my self-care and spiritual practices.

During the phone conversation my friend, Susan, beeps in on the other line. As soon as I finish with Sam I call back Susan who has been a long time member of our community. She tells me that she has just purchased a home in the Smoky Mountains of North Carolina and invites me to use it whenever I want. It seems no one will be using it for the month of February, so I jump at the chance. This is the very thing I have been asking for. The mountains have been calling me. This is the very thing that will give me the shot in the arm I am looking for after a demanding couple of years.

The transformation of my mother and our home has transformed us as well. You can't help change after a loved one passes on. No one tells you how much upheaval there will really be when you tear apart your home for several months. Even though mother's passing was good for her, the remodeling looked great, and we were ready for transformation, it required more of us than we expected.

I am so excited to get away and have some time by myself. This news gets me through the busyness of the holidays. I tell everyone I meet where I am going. Some of them think I am nuts and kindly smile. I live in Florida and I am excited to be going North in winter? It's definitely not everyone's cup of tea.

February arrives and it seems this is one of the worst winters ever in the country, even more so in the mountains of North Carolina where I am headed. It's been 25 years since I lived in the north, so I am naïve about what lies ahead. My friend warns me to listen to the weather reports and stay in touch with her neighbor for more detailed updates about conditions on their mountain. I don't give the weather another thought until I get closer and then reality sets in.

When I first call, Adam, her neighbor, is not so hopeful I can even get onto her road especially with new storms coming in. I wait extra days, and visit my sister, Nancy, and her family, who I haven't seen for awhile in Columbia, South Carolina, which is on the way.

Day 1 - Friday

Finally, it seems there may be a window of opportunity for me to get there. I am three hours out. As I get close to Asheville, North Carolina, the snow has already begun to fall. Thank God my friend has stocked up on basic food items and invited me to use whatever is there. I did do some shopping at one of my favorite stores, Trader Joe's, while I was waiting in Atlanta. I had planned on making one more stop for perishables when I got close, but that is not going to happen. I will have to make do with what I have.

I follow my Mapquest directions and encounter a flashing detour sign that says the road is closed ahead because of fallen rocks. This could put a major kink in my plan. In the mountains, a detour can mean lots of extra driving. Since, I have no backup plan, I just keep on driving for as long as the road lets me, which surprisingly takes me where I need to go. Even so, I am definitely rattled by what could have been and the pressure to arrive at my destination.

In my confusion, I get off the freeway one exit too soon, which disorientates me even more. I stop at the nearest service station, take a moment to breathe and go at it again. This time I am successful. I find the right streets and soon begin the big climb up the mountain. Snow begins to accumulate as I make my ascent. I am so grateful for front wheel drive and two new front tires, but I soon find out that these amenities are useless.

I drive upward, winding around one turn after another, some of which are hairpins. As it begins to get slippery, my Wisconsinite instincts kick in after years of being buried. I talk my car up the hill, reassuring it that it is doing a good job, and that we are too close to give up now. My confidence deflates as I pass an abandoned, snow covered car pulled over to the side of the road. I push on.

I have taken the car as far as it will go without changing gears. Now I must call upon more extreme measures, and I am forced to put my car in the lowest possible gear. It has been 39 years since I took driver's education; therefore I am not even sure that I can do what I am doing without blowing my transmission. I don't know my car that well. There's no time to call and ask my husband for advice and my situation would only put him in a panic. No time to read the manual either. I have to keep on going. I am inching my way, slipping and sliding as I go. Finally, I see the street sign to Susan's house. I breathe a sigh of relief! I am almost there. *Thank you God.*

At the corner, a teenager walking with a shovel comes up to my window and says, "I am surprised the road is really not that bad." I take that as another vote of confidence and make a sharp turn which takes me down a hill. I drive past another abandoned car, which makes me even more nervous this time since the road turns into one lane. Passing the vehicle is almost impossible.

I slowly make my way around and head up an even larger slope. I still have no idea how far I have to go. I get stuck halfway up this hill. I back down carefully and go at it again, getting farther but not far enough. At this point, I am spent, quite unnerved by the whole predicament and yell out to myself, "What the hell are you doing? You have a life and a family.

Why are you here? Why are you putting yourself and your car in harm's way?" I wanted a new car, but I really don't want to destroy this one along with myself on this mountain for that matter. I back up again and this time park my car in front of the one at the bottom of this slope and sit there. What to do next? I take a big, deep breath.

For the first time I have a chance to really see and appreciate the Winter Wonderland around me. It has been years since I have seen such beauty. The mountain and trees are snow covered and more continues to fall. It is so peaceful and quiet. I decide to start walking and find my friend's house on foot. I walk to the top of the hill and at long last there it is at the end of the road. Now, I just need to get my car up the steep slope and I am in the clear. I don't even care if I am stranded for days. This is exactly what I asked for.

I open the house and marvel at her beautiful accommodations that were to be my home for the next nine days and gave thanks that I am safe. I'm finally here.

There are still a few jobs that have to be done before I can relax. For one thing, my car is blocking the road which leads to another neighbor's house. I call Adam, Susan's neighbor across the road, whom I've been talking to, and we meet outside. He tries to drive my car up the hill, and I gladly let him, relieved to let someone else take over. He has much more experience with snow and ice after all. I didn't know how much more of this I could take at this point. I'm gutsy, but this was definitely over the top for me. Normally, I feel very young for my age, but now I am feeling tired and old.

Adam manages to get my car even higher and thinks he can back down a little more to make the final summit. Unfortunately, when he does, the car gets stuck in the accumulating snow on the side of the road. Together we shovel away snow under the tires and try again and again to break free. It isn't until another neighbor comes that we are able to get the car unstuck, back on the road, and toward the house. Adam is the one who makes the final climb. The dead end of the road is the perfect place for my car to sit and sit it will for the next 9 days. I am so grateful to the two guys who made all this possible. That day I was grateful to all the men in my life who have more guts than I do when it comes to bad weather conditions and cars.

I take my time carrying my own luggage up the snowy driveway. There is no way I am going to ask the neighbor for more help after all he has done. After more treks through the snow, my necessary luggage is in the house. I thought it would be time for relaxation until I discover the water isn't running. It was suppose to be turned on before I got there. Could the pipes be frozen or is it the well? I call my friend. For the night, I have what I need. She has containers of water stored for emergencies.

Day 2 - Saturday

This morning my friend calls and assures me that the water problem will be solved. I appreciate her confidence and follow instructions from the well expert. I declare to myself before heading outdoors, "I am in the flow!" I want to see water flowing. After all the blockage occurred on my time. Inside I turn the circuit breakers off for the water heater and pump. Outside, as I endure the cold, I take out all the insulation around the well, disturb the nice warm home of a little mouse, hook up my blow dryer to an extension chord and blow warm air over it until it thaws.

Thankfully, Adam, who drove my car up the hill the day before and parked it safely, shows up to see how I am doing. Shortly after, the water starts to flow. How I love water! I would not have been able to stay here without it. He tells me I could get a job unfreezing wells. I think to myself, I have that going for me. Once again, I appreciate his support.

Finally, it is Saturday afternoon and I think it is now time for the retreat portion of my week to officially begin. Everything is working, and this is the moment I have been waiting for. I get to do whatever I want, and there is no schedule. I can eat whatever I want, whenever I please. I can sleep as long as I like. I only have to take care of myself. I decide to give myself the weekend off from writing and relax. My body is sore from carrying my luggage and walking up and down the steep driveway. Furthermore, living at sea level and subtropics doesn't prepare you for high altitudes and freezing temperatures.

I bring a few of my favorite movies to enjoy. With the flip of a switch, there is nice fire going in the fireplace. I am warm and cozy. I get some snacks lined up and find I can't get the DVD player to work. My friend told me she didn't have all the technology worked out yet with her satellite dish. She just recently moved in. I don't want to bother her with one more thing so I read up on it the best I can. I still can't figure it out. I go to Plan B. I turn on my laptop thinking that I have played CD's on it before. The message on my laptop says I don't have a player to play the

DVD. I give in thinking, "Okay, I am not here to get lost in movies. I said I wanted quiet time to listen so okay *Spirit, I am listening.*

Days 3 and 4 - Sunday and Monday

The next two days I do my spiritual practices, visioning, reading, and listening to CD's. I go outside, even though the temperature is only in the mid 20's just to get a breath of fresh air and some exercise. The view of the mountains is beyond words. I spend much of my time just staring out the window at the magnificent Smoky Mountains before me.

It is definitely quiet. I am hearing quite well. I hear every little creak there is inside and out. A paperclip, literally, could drop anywhere in the house and I would hear it. I hear the crash of icicles fall from the roof as the sun melts them from the previous days accumulation of snow.

The evenings are hard. At home, this is the time when things really get crazy at our house, making dinner, getting Joseph, our son, to one practice or another. Here, I put the TV on at dinner time just to hear people's voices and to feel like I am a part of the world. This helps a lot. I like quiet. This is very quiet. I feel like I have the hearing range of a dog. Now I understand why people leave their TV's on for their pets. It makes them feel more comfortable. I feel comforted by the noise.

When the sun goes down, it's black. The only lights are city lights off in the distance and the ones I have on inside. During the day it doesn't matter that there are no window coverings on the windows or doors. At night the picture changes completely. I feel like a fish in a fish bowl. Anyone can see in if they were standing outside. I knew going that could be an *issue* for me but I was so determined to have time away I figured I would deal with it. Really how bad can it be? I'm in the mountains surrounded by trees with neighbors nearby yet not close enough to see. I'm 4,000 ft. above sea level, almost to the top of a very high mountain. It's 11 degrees at night. The street is buried in snow. Who is going to get me? What is possibly going to happen that will put me in danger?

Normally, I am fearless. I do things others wouldn't think of doing. I can hardly be considered a lightweight. My strength is helping people face all kinds of problems, seeing problems for the illusion that they are and getting to the heart of the matter. This little "thing" is beginning to get to me.

Day 5 - Tuesday

On the night of the fifth day, the perfect storm of another kind comes together. I stay in all day because it is so cold. My car is still snowed in so I am not going anywhere. I don't exercise which would have helped blow off any neurotic energy. Cabin fever starts to take me over. I don't realize until the next day when I assessed the situation that all the teas I brought were caffeinated. On top of that I had bought myself some chocolates for dessert…more caffeine. Those are really just poor excuses for something deeper going on in me.

By evening, even watching the inspirational athletes courageously performing their events for the Winter Olympics in Vancouver doesn't help. Something is building and it chose now to surface. I can't help but imagine that someone is going to walk up the outside stairs to the deck and then what will I do? It didn't matter that the stairs are deep in snow. My thoughts continue to grow into fearful ones. Turning on the outside lights helps a little. At least, then I can see what was there. Even so, I am alone with myself.

What concerns me most are that my thoughts are spiraling downward. I am out of control. I think back to what this was all about. I have overcome quite a few fears throughout the years so at first I am unsure as to what is causing all this. I remember a point in my life where I was extremely vulnerable, immersed in victim consciousness. I am in my early 30's and I attract on three different occasions over a period of several years, a man approaching me from behind in a park, putting a knife to my throat, being followed in a crowded mall and being watched through a window in my apartment early one morning.

I had to take a look at that. It didn't matter that they happened long ago or that I was now in my mid-fifties and not as desirable sexually. The experiences were still real to me and came to the surface under the extreme conditions in which I had placed myself.

I begin asking myself, "Is this the real reason for being here?" I thought it was to work on my book and relax, now I have this going on. This seems to be a huge block keeping me from enjoying my time. I knew I needed to be free of this feeling, but how?

Adding more pressure to the already intense situation, I think about how powerful my thoughts have become. I have lived the last 25 years believing that I am first cause to my experience, that I am a cocreator with Life, that I attract conditions, experiences and people into my life by the power of my thoughts, that I am 100% responsible for what happens to me whether it is something I am consciously or unconsciously aware of. This way of thinking and believing has been extremely empowering to me and I have seen great results from it. Knowing all this and teaching it for the last 17 years, I am surprised to find myself in the thick of it. Here, I am writing a book called, *I Can Do This Thing Called Life: and So Can You!* and now I am being faced with a personal challenge that is getting the better of me. How can you write a book with a title like that if you can't do this? There was something more to face that I hadn't properly taken care of at the time.

I discover the real reason I am here is to face myself, to see all there is to see, to have the courage to look my fear in the eye and really know what is there, know what is still getting in the way of me being more. It didn't take long for that fear to show up and when it does, it comes on full force. I need a way to get through being afraid.

That same evening, my oldest son, Nick, calls from Portland to talk in the midst of my breakdown. He is his happy, bubbly self. His voice alone is the reassurance with reality that I need. Thank God, I am not completely cut off from the world: I have cell phone coverage. I am happy to hear his voice. He doesn't call often and yet he knows when to call. I give him an overview of what is going on, skimming the surface of it so he won't think his mother is going over the edge.

One of his specialties is Ho'oponopono, the ancient Hawaiian healing method by Dr. Hew Len who healed patients on a mental ward by looking at the names on their files and repeating over and over again, *I love you. Please forgive me. I am sorry. Thank you.* (More information about it under Spiritual Practices later in the book). Nick is quite the expert. We both have found it extremely helpful in washing away past memories.

During our conversation, Nick shares a personal story of how he recently used Ho'oponopono while thinking of someone he was having difficulty with in his life. While, it was a great sharing, more importantly to me was the timing of his call and the message he left with me. Here I am having trouble staying calm and keeping my thoughts out of fear so I decide to use Ho'oponopono on myself. *That was it. This is something I can do immediately.*

I thank him for the reminder and as soon as we hang up, I crawl into a comfortable chair, close my eyes and say to myself, "I love you. I forgive you. I am sorry. Thank you." I love you for who you are, perfect and imperfect, complete and incomplete all at the same time. I forgive you for ever having seen yourself as a victim, as incapable, as unsafe. I am sorry in the presence of God. Thank you for clearing and cleaning these very old memories that need to be released in me".

I repeat the words over and over again and almost instantly find relief. I can breathe again. From there, I see the visual of a fountain of love coming up from within me, pouring out its endless love. I become the fountain. I am filled with love. The love pours out into the room, the house, outside surrounding the house and beyond. I find myself saying the words, *I Can Do This.*

I reflect that it was my *mind* that played the same old stories over and over making things worse. It was love and focus on my *heart* that pulled me out of what my head could not. My heart called me to the mountains and called me to a cleaning and clearing in me so that I can experience more love for myself and others. My experience was not going to be healed intellectually; however it took my mind to focus on a greater idea so that I could get in touch with my heart.

After a few hours of sleep, I wake up. There is so much going on in my mind regarding what had just happened. I have to write, take my power back. This fear is over once and for all. I am determined that the remaining five days in the mountains will be great and that I will get whatever other realizations I need to get before I leave. It feels good to be me. This experience leaves me feeling more comfortable in my own skin. The mountains are there for me, wrapping their arms around me. I enjoy the love and support of Spirit. I feel stronger, more powerful than ever. I am determined to keep this attitude and enjoy the rest of my time fully and I do.

Day 6 - Wednesday

I rest, write and take in as much as I possibly can of what happened the evening before.

Day 7 - Thursday

I call some friends who moved to the area from our spiritual community. I want to see them while I am in their vicinity. They come to get me for a visit. They pick me up at the end of my street so they won't get stuck. It feels so good to be off the mountain, being with people you care about, eating good, fresh food that I almost don't want to go back. They drop me off at nightfall and I start walking up the one lane road that leads me to my home away from home. It is very dark. This isn't so bad. I feel safe compared to when I had my episode of fear just days ago. I look up to a sky full of bright, shining stars and a striking sliver of a moon. It is breathtaking. I almost don't want to go in. I have a chance to see things from the outside in.

Day 8 – Friday

On Friday, I take my weekly call with my treatment partner, Sam. With his help, I see that this may not be the place where the major writing is to take place. More importantly, this experience is necessary for me to write for the beginning of my book.

Albert Einstein wrote, "I think the most important question facing humanity is, 'Is the universe a friendly place?'" Everyone has to answer that question. Our world is so immersed in fear, we are afraid to move. We are afraid to be ourselves. We are in fear of who we are and what we can do. It is a very old, unhealthy story we have been telling ourselves for generations.

It's true even for me. Situations come up unexpectedly in everyday life and my mind begins to play the old story where someone is out to get me or take something that belongs to me, having me believe I live in an unfriendly, unsafe world. I stop and ask myself over and over again, "Is that true?" "Do I believe I live in a friendly universe?" This question straightens me out immediately and aligns me with the way I choose to live. *Yes, I live in a friendly universe and there really is nothing to fear. There is no evil so there can only be good. What seems evil to us is simply a lack of love.*

When I think this way, I see and feel the love of others around me. I know that people are good and that they want to do right. Any evidence to the contrary is just a reflection of their own hurt and pain.

During our phone conversation, Sam also strongly suggests that I go out, lie in the snow and look up at the sky, to feel the connection with Mother Earth. Later that day, I do what he suggested and feel one with the mountain. The ground is solid and the sky vast. I relax into myself. I even make an angel in the snow.

Following his call, I talk with my friend, Ann, whom I met the previous year on a trip to Tanzania with our mutual friends, Kathy Hamilton and Floyd Hammer, founders of Outreach Africa. She asks me what is going on and I tell her about my breakthrough. She then told me that for her 50th birthday, she decided to spend a weekend alone on their sailboat and how she had to face some fears about her safety. The normally locked entrance to the marina was open and the lock on the door to her cabin was broken. She moved through her experience and enjoyed her time alone. *What some of us will do for some time alone!*

I appreciate her daring spirit and remember another example of her strength and courage. It was her birthday while we were in Tanzania. She had an opportunity to go out with the water team to a remote village in the middle of nowhere and teach the villagers how to produce chlorine and purify their own drinking water. I remember her saying that even though it was so desolate and wild, she never felt so free. We pay a price to live close together in a community. There are lots of advantages. We feel safer in numbers. We also give up some of our freedom and independence, our space. We even loose touch with who we are, and how to follow our own natural instincts. We become more dependent on those around us and less dependent on our own inner guidance. Sometimes it feels good to be with ourselves in nature. It is empowering to know we are capable enough to stand on our own, we belong and that we are a part of a greater picture, the Universe, ITself. My experience, here, during this time has helped me appreciate how much I have matured. Later that same day, I decide to venture out. I am feeling mentally and physically strong. I decide to extend my walk and go further up the mountain, maybe even to the top. Along the way, a voice calls out. I meet an older gentlemen, Norman, who invites me inside out from the cold into his house. We talk and for the next couple of days, he and his dog, Sasha, give me a tour of the area which is also very beautiful.

With each moment, I feel more and more like I belong to the world again. I feel the support all around me. Adam, the neighbor across the street, calls to say he is there to help get me leave when the road conditions get better. By the end of the week, the temperatures warm up, and melting begins. There's my perfect chance to get out when I need to head back home.

I am so grateful for this journey into myself. I know I am stronger because of it. This is the best Valentine's Day present I can give myself. My friend gave me the best present she could have given me with the use of her home. My husband gave me the best present by taking over the responsibilities at home and at work. Love, eventually, took over and cleared up some old fears.

My friend, Ann, also shared with me in our conversation a line from the movie, *Defending Your Life* starring Meryl Streep and Albert Brooks. She had no idea that was the very reason I brought that movie with me was to once again review the ending. But, I didn't have to see it because she gave me what I wanted: the ending words where the defender says,

> *I feel he has sufficiently passed the fears that would keep him from being a remarkable citizen of the universe. I've wholeheartedly recommended full onward movement.*

These words are music to my ears. The Universe is speaking through her to me. I believe we are all here to conquer our fears that keep us from being remarkable citizens of the universe, so that we can embrace full onward movement.

Now, when I think back to my experience in the mountains, I know I really was extremely protected. Nothing could have hurt me. I was so loved and provided for. I was put in a very safe place, like a baby in a padded playpen, where I could face myself and my fears, and work things out.

Love restored me to wholeness on the mountain. Love will move you through whatever you are facing, too, and make you whole again, as soon as you are ready.

Now let's consider, A World That Works for All.

I Can Do This Thing Called Life and So Can YOU!

2
A World That Works for All

There are two ways to live your life…one is as though nothing is a miracle. The other is as though everything is a miracle.

Albert Einstein

A couple of years ago, my husband, John and I were coming back from a short getaway in St. Augustine, celebrating our 15th wedding anniversary. We had a great time walking around the streets of the oldest city in North America, shopping, eating at garden restaurants with delicious foods, enjoying a warm, gorgeous spring, with beautiful flowers and fragrances. We were heading back home to Orlando where our grown daughter, Liz, was taking care of our son, Joseph.

On the way, we decided to see the beach one last time. For convenience, we picked one you could drive on. We arrived at the entrance to find a sign that said only 4 by 4's allowed. John and I had a van. We wanted to see the ocean so badly we could taste it. Because we live inland, we take advantage of those times we are close. The magnificent ocean was in full view before us. John drove up to the guard at the entrance and asked him about the conditions. He agreed only 4 X 4 vehicles were recommended. He also said, "I'm not going to stop you from going on although you most likely won't make it".

We were feeling so good that we decided to chance it. We drove onto the beach without much of a problem, had a nice walk, and decided to head back. Filled with the ocean air and mesmerized by the beauty all around us, we missed several signs saying there was no exit back to the way we entered. We proceeded to plough ahead and predictably got stuck. There was nothing we could do.

Two men came along and tried to push us out with no success. The van didn't budge. Quite a bit of sand had accumulated going off the beach and there was a slight incline leading to the road. Now I was even wondering how we ever got on the beach to begin with. Obviously there was no stopping us at the time; indeed, maybe we weren't as excited about heading home and ending our time away together.

I remember thinking this could not be happening to us. The beauty of the days could not end on this note. One guy that helped told us this happens all the time. Hearing that there were others who had not taken the well intentioned advice made us feel better. He said someone will be coming with a 4-wheel drive vehicle and be able to get you out. There is always help. I was grateful for his assuring words that helped calm me. Someone would have to do something soon because we were blocking the entrance. New arrivals had to back up and go to another entrance. *How embarrassing.* Help was still nowhere in sight. Where do we go from here?

John walked back to the beach to see if he could find help there, which was the perfect time for me to get mentally focused. I knew our fears were getting in the way of our help coming. Getting quiet inside my self was definitely in order. I had to get the ego stuff out of the way.

Yes, the support we needed was right there even if I couldn't see it yet. We always have everything we need right where we are because the Infinite is always present. IT is perfect Intelligence. IT knows what IT is doing in each and every situation. I treated to know we were supported; a power that creates universes can surely help get us out of this little jam. What's the worst that could happen? We would have to pay to have the car towed?

The spiritual universe is all about flow, movement, and circulation. Being a part of all that is, the physical universe is about that as well. We get in the way of our flow when we see ourselves separate from what is going on, spiritually, or cut off from our Source in some way. Reality hit and I began to feel stupid that we had not listened to the warnings and instead insisted on having our way.

Once I acknowledged my feelings, I was able to let them go. By staying present in the moment, I was able to get myself back in alignment with Infinite Intelligence. Focusing my energy and attention on the past, (what we did wrong) or the future (what will happen next) put me out of alignment. I took my power back and knew we were in the flow and taken care of.

During the short time I closed my eyes to mediate, the idea came to me that someone had the need to give someone else help today as much as we had the need to receive it. I finished my mental work, opened my eyes and saw two new 4-wheel drives waiting before me. John approached from his walk with another guy who said all he needed was a rope. A rope was produced by the driver of an oncoming vehicle and everyone went to work. The rope was attached to the front of our van so the 4-wheel drive vehicle could pull. John and another guy pushed the van from behind. We were out of there in no time.

The World is Wonderful

The world really is a wonderful place when you see it the way it really is from a spiritual point of view. We were so supported. Everyone worked together and did their part. No one laughed at us or called us stupid. They might have thought so but they didn't go there. They were kind and helpful. Infinite Intelligence didn't go there either. We weren't punished or rejected for making a silly move.

Not only were there the obvious natural consequences of sand on a beach, there were the consequences of me being out of alignment with our divine nature. Not feeling good about yourself or your decisions puts you out of the flow because you are not being true to your divine nature, which is always good. I had to love and forgive myself and John in order for me to reestablish the peace and harmony within my being that would open the doors for help.

Seeing myself as a powerful creator and not as a victim also puts me in alignment with what is true about me. There are choices and decisions John and I made together that day that caused our predicament. Recognizing the nature of Life, and how IT works, that we are always working with a power greater than ourselves, got in motion the chain of events that set us free.

We are all really so loved and supported. When we see the world as rigid, fixed, set in stone, unchangeable, we experience the world in a limited way. When we believe things can only happen a certain way or that we are on our own facing the world by ourselves, life will reflect that belief back to us and that will be our experience. When we see circumstances, conditions and physical appearances as reality, they become so. They very well may be a current fact in our lives, but they are not necessarily reality as it is from a higher, spiritual perspective.

When we see our world view as spiritual and everyone in it as spiritual beings and that we have a relationship together that goes beyond this dimension, then we will see and experience the world of infinite possibilities. That's where things start getting really interesting.

It's An Inside-Out World

Typically, we believe that the world is solid and unchangeable and adapt ourselves accordingly. There are some situations and conditions we have lived with all our lives. We have problems we believe we are stuck with for life. We live our lives from the outside-in, letting the outside determine how things will be for us, parents, partners, friends, colleagues, coworkers: the world. We think that when those around us change or this problem gets solved, we will be happy and our life will be good.

That's part of the frustration. It's not that way at all. It's really an inside-out world. It is a spiritual world, not just a physical one. The physical one is the result of the spiritual. I know that sounds funny, but everything that is going on with our thoughts and beliefs, the conversation we have going on in our heads all day long determines how our life will go. Everything that goes on inside of us determines the experience we are having on the outside. Everything really begins within us. Personally and collectively, our thoughts and beliefs play out into our experiences. Just as we were a perfect idea in Universal Mind before we were created, everything in our lives was first an idea or a belief we had that played out in the physical world as an object, a person, a situation, a condition, or an opportunity.

Two Ways to Live

Oriah Mountain Dreamer writes of the voice that whispers our name: "Always it says: Wake up my love, You are walking asleep. There's no safety in that!"

There are two ways to live: unconsciously and consciously. Unconsciously we run around doing, doing, doing, not even realizing what we are doing or why. We live in the dark not really knowing what is going on around us, accepting what we see as the only thing that is real. We fail to see the Universe as Infinite Intelligence or expansive in what IT knows and can do. We identify ourselves with our small, "i" self, the human, personality self, always on a schedule, not enjoying life and struggling to keep up or even stay in the game. Being unconscious is a safe state for us to go into when the world gets to be too much to handle.

Conscious living means living from a place where we are awake and aware of the many things going on around us. Being aware of different levels of experience happening simultaneously such as physical and spiritual, mental and emotional, hidden meanings, seeming coincidence are all examples of conscious living. In order to appreciate the many different things happening for a reason, we are required to build our capacity by being more conscious, bringing our full attention to what is going on before us. Even though we practice living consciously, there are times when we check out. We have had enough. It's difficult to have full awareness all the time.

Living consciously requires effort. It takes work for us to be present in the now, to be able to put all else on hold, and enjoy the moment, and to see ourselves and all others as connected and living the one Life together. Being conscious requires listening, looking someone in the eye when we communicate, taking in information from more than just our senses, reading our hearts, following our inner guide, trusting feelings, taking time to *be* and enjoy life. Living this way increases the life experiences for all involved and supports the idea of a world that works for all.

Living Under the Law of Averages

We all live under the Law of Averages. Under this law, you are going to win some and you are going to lose some in Life. The average life experience is just that, "average". Sometimes you get lucky and sometimes not so lucky. Some days are good and some not so good. The "average" life experience is not as great as you might think. You can wait your whole life for something really good to happen. Patience is required. That gets boring very quickly. We have an experience and we react to it. We talk about how bad something is or how difficult it is for us to have a particular problem, how someone is out to get us, or life, specifically, has it in for us. Our thoughts and attention are focused on the negative, and we talk about how bad things are going with whoever will listen.

Sometimes our minds are so focused on what happened years ago, we won't let ourselves forget. We create a monument representing it so we will always remember. Sometimes we are so focused on what is presently going on, we can't move beyond it. Other times, our thoughts are centered on what the future might bring. We can't help but remain emotionally charged with thoughts of going down the tubes, with sickness, disease, financial ruin, abandonment, joblessness, and other afflictions. We believe our vigilance is required to keep it all at bay otherwise it is sure to happen to us. After all, it's happening all around us to people we know and love. Stories abound everywhere you go. The news informs us daily of how bad things can get.

These negative issues play so heavily on our consciousness that we even believe we are dodging bullets everyday. One might say, thank God it wasn't me or my family that had this problem. We believe that sooner or later, one or more of those situations will happen to us as well, because life is looked at as a game of chance.

This is who we are and how it is. It's hard to convince us otherwise. When we live under the Law of Averages, all we can possibly do is relive more of the same in our lives. It can be very frustrating to get through a situation only to attract it again and again. Usually, the players involved are different and the scenario has changed; however if you look closely, you will recognize that you have been there before.

This is how most of the world has lived up to this point in evolution. Conditions are happening around the world, or affect us directly and we react to them. We are reactors to life instead of being active participants in it or creators of it. Life keeps coming at us and we try our very best to cope. Our experience keeps repeating itself because *we* haven't changed. We are in need of a better idea of ourselves, and for lives in order for us to break out of living under the Law of Averages. When we believe life is happening outside of our control, the quality of our lives and experience is determined by others. There has to be another way.

Living Under the Law of Cause and Effect

There is another way to live that overrides the Law of Averages. Living under the Law of Cause and Effect places us in a completely different paradigm or way of looking at life. It puts us in the driver's seat. We still get the benefit of the Law of Averages *and* we increase our opportunities by deciding to take charge of our own lives. We can be proactive and see the beauty of life around us and cocreate with the Infinite even more. Whatever we can imagine in our minds, we can manifest for ourselves. The sky is the limit.

We begin living under the Law of Cause and Effect when we begin to see that thoughts really are things. When we change the way we are looking at the physical world, we change our experience. Everything we see and know began first as someone's idea. Just like the entire universe and all of us have been made by an Infinite Creator, we are the creators of our own circumstances and life. What we are thinking about is being projected into material form. The only way to move under the Law of Cause and Effect is to change our approach from a reactionary one to a proactive one otherwise we live by default taking what we get. Seeing the good in what is happening all around us is a perfect place to start.

We are not the conditions or circumstances we are experiencing. No matter how good they seem, we are something so much more: We are spiritual beings. We are greater than the thoughts we have. We are greater than our bodies, our work, our lives. There is a thinker behind the mind that is thinking. We can actually watch and observe ourselves in the very drama we have created, which helps us see that there is much more to us than we thought before.

The Law of Cause and Effect surpasses the Law of Averages. We may still win some and lose some accordingly to averages and completely override them in others. We take our lives to another level by beginning to see that we are first cause to our experience. Everything begins with us. We can be master of our own life. We don't have to be a statistic. We can decide to live healthy and well. If we are creators of our experience then we are responsible for what is happening to us. As we change the thoughts we are having about ourselves and life, as we open ourselves up to greater wisdom and understanding about how Life really works, we begin to play in a much bigger game.

Beings of Great Desire

We are beings of great desire. We were never meant to sit and wait or to be bored with the present state of things. We were meant to create good all around us. Desiring more is not a bad thing. Seeking more is usually misinterpreted as wanting more material things. It's not things we crave as much as we yearn for a greater experience of ourselves. It's not that we can't enjoy material goods, too…we can. What we really desire is to have a more fulfilling and enjoyable life experience. Our heart wants us to get in touch with our infinite selves. What we seek is to connect with the Infinite and work together with the way of Life instead of against the grain. Our desires are given to us by Life, ITself wanting to express and experience ITself more in the physical. We are the way IT experiences ITself in the land of form.

We set ourselves free when we take our power back from those we have given it and embrace a larger idea of who we are.

Those are the kinds of shifts in perception we are being called to make if we indeed want to experience more than we have so far. Many are ready to take their lives and their world to another level. You may very well be one of them.

The World Keeps Getting Better

The process of unfoldment and evolution of our human race continues, making things better and better through time. The world really is becoming a more loving and accepting place. New generations bring the total accumulated consciousness of the human race with them when they are born. That means they are aware, at least on a deeper level, of the worst of the worst and the best of the best of human consciousness. We see their level of intelligence. They are stronger, more present, clear, and focused beings than we are. They are fresh from Spirit. They know who they are because they haven't been buried by a past or experiences that have helped them forget. Sometimes we have difficulty working with them because we don't have the real picture of who they are as pure spirit.

Many of us are brought up believing that we have to educate the new generations. It is our responsibility to train them, and to impart them with knowledge. Children are empty vessels. It is our job to teach them what they need to know and how to love. What we don't know or forget is that these beings come into our world as pure love. They are created out of love and intelligence. Love and intelligence is at the heart of who they are. They are powerful creators in a smaller body. It is our job to love and support them as they find their way in the world. As disheartening as it may sound to some, they have more to teach us than they have to *learn from us*.

As we watch our children and admire the freshness of Spirit that they are, we are reminded of who we are as Spirit and inspired to be young again in our own thinking and the way we live. In reality, it's not looking young as much as feeling good knowing who you are and living life the way it was meant to be lived. It's never too late for us to remember we are spirit and recreate ourselves and our lives.

Change is Good

So many changes our going on in our world today, and the speed with which they are happening is astounding. It really is enough to make your head spin. On top of change, we are living during a time when things seem to be falling apart faster than they are coming together. Companies falling apart, layoffs, downsizing, financial ruin are a few examples. While that may be frightening and bring up intense fear, thinking about changing the life we know, especially when we are forced into it, is it possible for us to believe something greater is at work?

Can we believe that our journey together into new, uncharted territory is a good thing?

Doesn't it make sense that the changes that are taking place are ones that must change in order for us to see a more loving world that works for all?

Can we believe that change is a part of life, in this world, and that there is an Intelligence behind it all that knows exactly what IT is doing?

Is it possible for us to view things from a higher place and see that all this *is* our next step on the evolutionary scale for our human species?

Is it possible for us to see that what goes up (new creations) must come down (old ones) in order to make way for the new?

Can we believe that there is a reordering or reorganization underway, and that it will be well worth any immediate or temporary inconveniences?

It's true we may not know how things will play out and what they will mean to us. That may make us feel uncomfortable. It may even mean that we are burdened with some drastic changes and detours in our own lives. If we have a strong relationship with Life, knowing we are always loved and supported where we are, then we can trust that we will not be led astray. The hand of God has been at work from the beginning of time. IT has successfully brought us to this point in our lives and is perfectly leading us now.

The nature of Infinite Intelligence has always been to create, and IT does this through you. Contrary to what some may say, Universal Mind is alive and well. IT continues to work with us individually and have IT's way with us all.

People Are Expressions and Extensions of Life

It has been said by some that the Earth is the perfect training grounds for evolving souls. How true. We are all unique expressions of the One and very different from one another. We are also at very different places with ourselves and various aspects of our lives. There can be no comparison. If we see life this way, there is no need for competition or comparison between people. We are all equal as spirit and on our own special path. If we see the way things really are, it helps us to be more kind and considerate of each other. Given the nature of life as it is currently in the world, it is a testament to the divine that we are able to get along as well as we do.

The world is going to do what the world is going to do. People are going to do what people do. One question we have to ask ourselves is, am I willing to wait to see what the world is going to do and then my life will be good? Another is, am I able to see my life as already good and create more of what I really want to experience? In other words, do I live in frustration with what is, or do I decide to get on with things by creating a better life for me and all those around me?

We don't have to wait for the world to change in order to find our happiness. We have taken things as far as they can go with the old paradigm. More is required of us to go further. We yearn to know ourselves more greatly, and we have the perfect opportunity to do that. If we want to take ourselves to a new level, we must decide to *Be* more.

A Spiritual Solution

We are being asked to look at things in a whole new way. Focusing on our problems only brings more of the same. Something has to change. We have been waiting for the world to change so that we can live better lives. We seem to find ourselves in the same boat over and over again without much improvement; and therefore we have to look at things from a different perspective.

A new way of living, a more spiritual way of life opens us up to a new possibility. This way asks us to come from a more loving and caring place which involves the care and support of all the life on this planet and the life yet to be for the generations to come. Decisions that we make today greatly impact future generations so we must consider how our current thought and actions will affect the future.

A great shift is underway affecting how we see and ultimately do things, like invest in our children, the environment, how we treat one another, how we think of ourselves. We are in the midst of a great transformation of consciousness within us and around us. What is taking place, internally, must play out as a new picture in the external.

While the many changes in the world may seem a bit unsettling, they are to be celebrated and encouraged because something greater is unfolding. We, ourselves are calling it into being. We've been waiting to see change all of our lives. We want things to be better. We are playing a part in the emergence of a whole new world. We want to live the life we were created to live. We want to experience ourselves as loving, prosperous, and successful beings. Fulfilling our purpose, doing what we love, doing what we came here to do is something we all desire at heart level. Something inside of us knows that a better way is possible, and it doesn't feel good to be out of alignment with that possibility. It's time for us to stop playing small and open the door to a new reality, the only Reality there is.

Whenever shifts take place internally, that change how we see things, every time we make an extra effort to reach out and help, every step we take toward personal growth, we are making a contribution to a grand creation together…a world that works for all. Whenever consciousness changes and our awareness grows, we expand our thoughts and beliefs, and the outer world changes to reflect those shifts in consciousness. It must. You absolutely cannot be moving on the inside without changes taking place on the outside.

This may seem like a new way to think for us. Throughout history, the great masters and avatars looked at life this way. This ancient wisdom has been available through the ages for whoever was ready to see it. What if, together with the Infinite, we could create the world of our dreams? That would be amazing, wouldn't it? Life really is quite incredible because it is there, waiting for us to believe in IT. As we move into alignment with the Universe by getting closer to understanding how Life really works, we see more and more that everything we could ever want is already here waiting for us.

What is Spiritual Living?

Spiritual Living is a deeper, more reflective, conscious, and more peaceful way of living. To live a spiritual life is to choose dedicating oneself to being a better person, who comes up with more loving solutions. Spiritual Living means supporting everyone and everything on the planet and beyond. To live spiritually means to feel more life and love. Living this way helps people to enjoy themselves because they are in touch with who they are as a spiritual being. Spiritual Living creates individuals who are at peace with themselves. To be spiritual means to love, honor and respect yourself. To live spiritually means to be happy with who you are. This way of life helps us to see ourselves as creators of productive, inspiring, and fulfilling lives.

Living spiritually means creating a firm, spiritual foundation from which to live and work. It is a proactive approach to life and means being present, having an awareness of what is possible, and spending time focused on creating a better life for ourselves. It means being actively engaged with Spirit in everything. We don't have to wait for something bad to happen and then pray or treat. Conscious or spiritual living means praying or treating, visualizing and visioning especially when we are feeling strong so we keep our focus on what is right and good, paying attention to the continuous impulses of Life directing and guiding us.

It means seeing ourselves as divine, a higher order of being.

Spiritual Living means to be respectful of all peoples, cultures, religions, traditions and countries whether we agree with them or not. It means to appreciate the diversity of life, knowing we are all living the one Life together, knowing all roads lead home.

It means to take 100% responsibility for our lives and what happens to them. Knowing the way we see ourselves and others plays a part in the quality of our relationships. Seeing perfection helps to bring it forth. Seeing good brings forth good.

It means people genuinely caring for one another, willing to give whatever they have because they know their connection with an Infinite Source that is always providing more.

This way of living means to support, encourage, uplift, inspire and love others in being all they can be. Everyone needs to know that there is someone in their corner no matter what.

Spiritual Living means taking ownership and responsibility for the care of Mother Earth, nature, our environment and treating it like it was our own because in Reality, it is. There is an Indian law that takes into consideration whatever action is being done and how it will affect those involved seven years from now.

It means participating in an ever-expanding and deepening relationship with the Infinite, whatever our definition or name of IT we have. We yearn to come home to the innermost being within, that place where we connect with all of Life.

It means to live a life we can be proud of, thereby leaving a legacy for others to enjoy. Mentorship or being a good example of what is possible is incredibly valuable for those who are following in our footsteps. Why not stand on the shoulders of giants and gain an even greater perspective and then pass it on?

This way of living requires us to use our precious minds for constructive thinking and creating, using our time, energy and love to create more of what we want to see.

Spiritual Living means showing up to life everyday, no matter what happened the day before, ready to give it our best. It takes great courage sometimes to show up to life especially during difficult times. Each day we do, we stand tall in our truth and prove that we are greater than any experience we have.

Living this way puts the emphasis on peace, creating interesting, unique, innovative ways to use what we have and share it with the world, working together, globally, as one human family enjoying our diversity and celebrating our unique perspectives.

It opens us up to being a clear channel for Universal Wisdom, thinking ideas that have never been thought before, appreciating our precious minds and even more the thinker behind them that determines our existence.

Spiritual Living sees each individual as a clear, open channel for good, a center of divine activity in the world.

Spiritual Living helps us to appreciate our bodies, their intelligence, complexity, balance and health, how responsive they are to us, how they support us as we move about the world.

It means making decisions that hurt no one and embrace the highest good of all. We can never go wrong coming from love. Life will support us as we consider what is best for all involved.

It means being dedicated to coming from the highest, most loving, abundant consciousness possible at all times. The greater our awareness and the bigger our perspective, the freer we become.

This is a Journey that begins within - within me, within You. So let's take a look at how that works.

I Can Do This Thing Called Life and So Can YOU!

3
Journey Into You

Sometimes I feel strong – like I'm growing and getting somewhere. Other times I feel so scared, insecure, so alone, so frustrated, so tired. Now I'm feeling frustrated, tired and depressed. I want to learn how to better myself, how to become more stable and secure within myself, to learn how to nourish myself without always running to someone else for acceptance and reassurance. I want these things badly – doing them is another story. I'm so afraid that I will never be able to accomplish this person I would like to become. Will I ever be satisfied with who I am or what I am doing or what I am experiencing? That scares me.

Cath Zokan(DePalma), Age 35

Love is the sole impulse for creation, and the man who does not have love as the greatest incentive in his life, has never developed the real creative instinct. No one can swing out in the Universal without love, for the whole Universe is based upon it.

Ernest Holmes

My good friends, Sam and Chris, and I formed a prayer trio years ago. It started as an idea to support our teacher, Dr. Kennedy Shultz, during his transition from this world. We loved him dearly especially since he had done everything for us. We were committed to knowing that the highest and best was happening for him now in his time of need. By that I mean knowing it was his time and his process was sacred to him versus catastrophizing or feeling sorry for him. Our time together evolved into a conference call every Saturday night to help us prepare as ministers for Sunday mornings with our communities, church business. It gave us an opportunity to vent, talk with others who really knew what ministry, specifically pulpit ministry, was like and all that comes with it. Together we brainstormed ideas, and supported one another in both work, and personal lives. It was a dynamic exchange. To top it off, we finished with a round robin mind treatment. (Reminder from the introduction: mind treatment or prayer treatment is affirmative prayer, a tool to shift our consciousness so that we can be in alignment with the mind of God or Universal Mind. See the chapter in section 3 for a more detailed explanation). Everyone took a turn stating the Truth from their own vantage point. These treatments encompassed the highest possibility that was happening for us and our communities.

One night Sam was unable to make the call. I was feeling exceptionally frustrated, out of my league with my work. Things didn't seem to be working. I didn't feel supported. I hated to say that because I knew that wasn't true. I just couldn't see it or feel it.

Chris said, "You know what your problem is Cath? You don't have an up close and personal relationship with God." It felt like a dagger to my heart. It split me right open. You know when you hear the truth because it stops you dead in your tracks. You can't ignore it even if you try. It was exactly what I needed to hear. He was absolutely right on. I was doing all the right things but not feeling any passion behind my work. There were so many things to do and details to remember while running a business. So much of what I was doing was not what I had come into this work for. I was not connecting at a deeper level to myself or my work and especially not to a higher power. It was true even though it hurt to hear. It was a powerfully, healing moment for me that I will never forget. Things were never the same again. This was a huge turning point for me. I knew where I needed to place my focus. I am forever indebted to him for calling it so clearly.

I grew up with the idea of a loving God. I believed God was more loving and kind than the elders would have me believe. Even still, it was hard to wrap my thoughts around this idea of how much I really was loved. For awhile, I abandoned the word "God" entirely, trying to break out of whatever perception I grew up with and was trapped in. It was difficult for me to see that I was worthwhile. I thought well of myself but obviously not well enough. There was so much more to me and I wanted to build a relationship with the Infinite.

Getting to Know Yourself

Recently, I found 20 or so tags from races I ran in the late '80's and early '90's in a file drawer in my office. Growing up, I had always been a little jealous of my brothers getting trophies for different sports. I didn't see myself as ever getting one. I don't remember if my grade school volleyball team won, and if so it would have been a group trophy. These race numbers were my trophies. Even though I completed every race, I was far from being fast. Some were 5K's and others were 10K's. I was reminded that I did have the discipline to get myself into shape. I spent the time required to mentally prepare and practice. I followed through on my personal commitments and goals for running.

There are moments when you remember events and experiences you have long forgotten. Going through pictures and memorabilia help you remember who you are, who you have been all along, accomplishments you have forgotten, reminders of your character, your good deeds, your highest hopes, your dreams and your heart's desires. All of this is part of getting to know yourself. Always remember that you are so much more than you appear to be.

You Are A Perfect Creation

One day on my walk through the park, a baby owl greeted me. I walked by the nest every week. There has been a nest there every spring for the last couple of years. This time a precious, wide-eyed, new being looked down at me. Because this is a first for me and such a rare event, I almost can't believe my eyes. It is a true gift from the Universe. I took steps to get different angles. The baby blended with the brown tone colors of the naked bark so well, I thought I was making this up and merely seeing a distortion in the bark. I have seen pictures of a baby owl peeking out from a branch so I have a visual of what that looks like.

However, I am 99.99% sure I am seeing right. I greeted the young one and told it how beautiful it was and that I was so happy it is here. We stared at each other for a long time and then, I let it be and went on with my walk.

As I got close to the end of my walk, I walked back to where I began. I glanced up at the tree one more time. The owl was gone. Maybe it was taking an early morning nap. Now I saw what the tree really looked like. The place where the baby was perched now looked empty and bare. Then something caught my eye on the branch above the nest, and I saw the wonder of Life sitting there in its perfection. I saw the whole baby owl, its downy feathers and intense, black eyes. We enjoyed another moment together. The Universe was staring and admiring ITself and IT's perfect creations "as us and" after 'creations' through us.

You, too, are a magnificent creation and expression of the Infinite. You are amazing, and beautiful beyond measure. Great riches lie within you. When you know who you are and appreciate what it is to be divine, it is easy for you to see that same goodness in others. To be fully alive and awake to yourself is quite a gift.

You are your most precious possession. You are the only one who will never leave you. You have a right to be here. You are so much more than you think you are. You are the perfection of Life unfolding perfectly and beautifully as you. You couldn't stop that from happening even if you wanted. Even if you resist that this is who you are, believing yourself to be less, Life will find a way for you to appreciate yourself. You can try and keep up the illusion that you are small and insignificant, not up to the task of living. You can keep convincing yourself and others that you don't know what you are doing. You can keep feeling like you are not enough, and thinking of yourself as a victim or that you are all alone with no help at all. You can live all that out in various experiences *or* you can decide to be who you really are and do what you came here to do: live life abundantly. Spirit is individualized and uniquely expressing as you.

While we enjoy getting the things we require and want, there is no greater, more permanent, more satisfying joy than getting to know ourselves as an infinite being. The river of Life runs deep in us, there is so much more to us than we ever knew. There will always be still more to discover about ourselves as infinite beings…to know we are one with all Life, one with our Source. That's why we are here.

It's Your Life

Everything begins with you…everything! You are the center of your world. The most precious relationship you have is the one you have with yourself. How you see yourself and treat yourself are both keys to how your life will play out. For instance, you may have been brought up to be humble, to think less of yourself and put other's first. That flawed thinking gets us into all kinds of trouble and sets us up for failure. Living humble is not in accord with Life's design for us. It places us out of alignment with our divine nature.

We are only held back by that which we believe we are stuck with. What we are stuck with is anything we are unwilling to deal with or face. Once we bring our full love and attention to our life or a particular aspect of our life and learn to make healthier choices, the picture will change.

Things are changing very rapidly in our world. Many people are pioneering a new way of living and thinking taking wisdom from all the great teachings and incorporating them into their own lives in a way that is meaningful to them. They are learning to listen and follow the guidance from the spirit within. More people are taking time to get to know themselves, to work on their own personal issues, to make mindful, more intelligent choices. They aren't jumping into marriage and having children just because the biological clock is ticking, or their parents want a grandchild. More consciousness, more maturity is needed behind our decisions and when it is there, we will experience greater depth to our lives.

Following your own path gives you greater freedom. You have time to discover yourself, find what you like and don't like, learn how to be self-sufficient, and do things your own way. We were not all meant to live the same exact life. Wouldn't it be great if people really knew who they were and knew what they wanted to make of their lives? The results could only be better than what they have been up to this point. The greater the freedom we have to follow our own path and create our own lives organically and naturally, the happier we will be.

I believe we are going to see more and more creative ways that people choose to live their lives. We are already seeing people work together, raising children. Different living situations, expanded relationships, creative ways of making a living are already underway.

The gift of Life is full of possibilities, full of potential, full of goodness, and we can choose to experience as much as Life has in store for us as we will allow. We were created from a perfect idea and allowed to experience ourselves for the god beings we really are to the degree that we open ourselves up to our divinity. The more we become open and receptive to the idea of being Spirit in form, the more satisfied we will be.

Your life is yours and my life is mine. When we see it this way, it helps us to understand that the way we think it should be is not the only way. There are many ways as there are people. Someone once said there are as many different religions as there are people; we all have our own perspective, our own interpretation. No two people think alike. This perspective gives us an appreciation for all the different ways that Spirit expresses as us all. This also helps us to be more loving, and respectful of the way others choose to spend their lives. Allowing everyone the freedom to be themselves will create a happier, more harmonious world. A more harmonious world gives us all greater freedom to enjoy our lives.

What About My Life?

Maybe you are just waking up, coming to, looking around and seeing what you have been missing. Some event has just taken place in your own life that has your attention. You just found out you have a health challenge, or you lost a loved one. The price of gas has tipped you off about things to come or you are no longer employed. The life you have been living no longer works the way you think it should, and seems to be falling apart faster than it is coming together; maybe the predictions of things to come have you in a panic. You may already be in over your head. Your darkest fears have already surfaced, and you can't see a way out.

Whatever it is, this is not the time to give up, run, hide or settle. It's not too late and it's never over. This isn't even the time to get angry, although there may be some exasperation. This is only the beginning. You were created for greatness. Life was meant to get increasingly better, richer, healthier and more loving.

Things happen in life even when you know everything you can possibly know. Sometimes we create situations that aren't so smart. Our mistakes don't have to be big; in fact, most of the time our mistakes are really small ones that when ignored, escalate.

The situation before you is not life-threatening even though it may feel like that. Once you realize what you are working with, you'll see it is not. Just ask, how big is my God or my idea of the Universe compared to my problem? In the grand scheme of things, our problems are very small even when they seem huge to us. It does help to get a larger perspective and to know that we can draw upon the greater Power at hand by recognizing IT's presence.

When life circumstances present themselves, celebrate the fact that you are being cleared out for something better and finally getting to the bottom of things. This is your chance to see things for what they really are, a learning experience. Trust and know that a way is being shown to you, that you will be guided. Be willing to surrender to the Higher Power even if you don't know how. Stay open. Listen for guidance. Believe that you are a part of a much greater Life and will be supported.

Now more than ever it is important that we keep our heads about us, stay focused on something greater happening, personally, and collectively, for our country and the world. Maybe your life is already good and you would like to make it even better. Whatever your situation is, it is important to keep your focus in the right way, put some spiritual practices in place. Learn to pray or treat, take up meditation, read something positive, write out your feelings, dreams and desires. It may be taking a walk in nature, camping out or fishing. It may be playing music or writing. Ultimately, you know what activities help you to feel better.

Priming the Pump

Spiritual practices are powerful. Sometimes when you first start, it doesn't seem that way. It takes a while to get going. Fortunately, there is no need to worry, the Infinite is always ready.

Zig Zigler, a very successful salesperson and trainer, has a great story about a man feeling thirsty and coming across an old pump in the woods. When he first pumped it, nothing *appeared* to happen. If you don't understand how a pump operates, you will think it doesn't work, and may get discouraged. Essentially, a pump has to be primed. Depending on when it was last used, it may need quite a bit of pumping before seeing results. Just because you don't see water the first few tries doesn't mean it's not there.

If he had stopped pumping and walked away when he got frustrated, he would have walked away thirsty, never knowing and never knew how close he came to seeing the steady stream of water possible. Because he stuck with it, he found refreshment, and the waters continued to flow without much additional effort on his part. Pumping once or twice regularly kept the water coming. He found he had more than enough.

The same is true with our prayers or mind treatments. We prime the pump by setting our intention. What would we like to see happen? What is our desire? Why is it important? Then, prime the pump and support that idea with our spiritual work. We keep pumping or affirming our truth until we begin to see it come into form. We continue to pray or practice mental treatment until we see the full picture of our creation. Our practices are a building process. They build our capacity. They prepare us to receive. (More about this in a future chapter).

Nothing we do in the way of spiritual practices is ever wasted even if we don't see or feel anything for a while. Everything we invest in ourselves in the way of betterment, especially our attempts to connect spiritually with our Creator, will pay off huge dividends in the long run.

What we do regularly comes in handy when we really need it. It doesn't even matter what our practices are as long as they feed you, and you feel better off by doing them.

Whatever keeps us centered, focused, empowered, inspired and engaged in life is worthwhile. Now more than ever with our faster paced living, world financial crisis, and increased weather activity happening in our world, to name a few, is a time we all need to be present, to stay conscious, to give our best love and attention to everyone especially ourselves. It is essential to our well-being and success. The larger the scope of our lives, and the more responsibilities we have, the greater the need for us to be centered and focused.

The Climb

A friend of ours, Frank Henninger, wrote a book called *Compass Points*. He writes of his first major climbing experience up Mount Rainier, in the state of Washington. He delves into discussions about the months of preparations beforehand, building his physical strength by carrying a backpack of rocks while walking for miles. There are mental preparations to make like psyching oneself up that you have what it takes to make the climb, to stay out in the cold and survive. Freezing, falling, breaking a limb, and even death are all part of what could happen when you decide to take on that kind of challenge. Descriptions of the actual experience describe difficulties with weather and visibility, keeping hydrated, having enough food, and eliminating, especially going from one building to a small hut in the middle of the night when temperatures are the coldest. In the middle of all that, Frank had a spiritual experience. Some realizations come to him that would not have unless one was under some kind of extreme condition. His story is a great study for approaching the seemingly impossible. The mountains are loved by many for their spectacular beauty but few people actually have the discipline and passion to prepare for a climb and make it happen.

I, too, love the mountains and even though I am not a mountain climber, I am in awe of them. I can relate somewhat, as I have had experiences in my life that felt like I was climbing a mountain. Some seemed insurmountable. Maybe you can think of some situations in your own life that are challenging. You may be going through a rough, grueling experience. You know what the goal is…the top of the mountain. You could turn back many times, as Frank did. Those around you think you are nuts and don't understand why you feel you have to climb a mountain, even less a most dangerous one. You have a good life. Why ask for trouble? Play it safe.

Even though you consult many experts about the climb, you are the only one that can make the decision to embark on the journey. If you haven't talked yourself out of it after listening to all the people who think you are crazy, and actually do it, you'll find the experience was more than just reaching the top and looking down at all the splendor and beauty. Something else happened along the way without you even noticing that is worthy of celebrating. This celebration is an inner one. You are not the same person you were when you first had the idea to climb. The adventure has made you into something more. It has grown you. Your capacity has become more than you ever thought possible and you feel an exhilaration that no one else can really know. You have achieved new heights of beingness.

As he was leaving, Frank's wife, Melody, gave him a note with an inspiration for him:

There is a point in our earthly existence where the visible begins to fade and our hearts have to follow a narrowly appointed road by faith. Being the substance of things hoped for, we travel into the mist with some trepidation, but nonetheless we are sure that our walk is based on the certainty of a fulfilled promise.

In our own lives, what we have known before fades away as we enter new, unknown territory. Even though we are anxious and afraid, all we have to do is keep on walking. We are guaranteed that good things will happen. Life has to support us because we are Life, too. IT has to support ITself. That's our path. That is our life. We must each go it alone and do our best.

Because of stormy weather conditions, Frank and his party were not able to reach the summit on the last day. Sometimes it isn't possible to reach your destination and there are times you will have to do it all over again as he later does. Life is a lot like that. It is important to pick the mountain you really want to climb because it will take all the strength you've got and more. However, the rewards become a part of you forever. There is a greater possibility waiting to be recognized and experienced by *you*. In experiencing those inner rewards and watching how magnificently Life works, you will get a better idea of how you can work together with IT, what your part is. You can learn to stop settling for less and keep the doors open to something better happening.

When you see that Life is happening all around you, you learn it's not really about the material possessions. Stuff is attractive to us for a time, as earthly beings. The fulfillment of our desires is really an invitation by Life to get to know ourselves better in a way that we didn't know ourselves before…to learn what we are really capable of on the way to manifesting what we need or desire in physical form.

Ernest Holmes, author of *Science of Mind* writes, "Spirituality is a constant, consistent attempt to feel the Presence of God in everything and in everyone", including ourselves.

Now, I invite you now to join me in looking at some specific areas of our lives, and explore just how "we can *do*" them.

"I Can Do This Thing Called Life and So Can YOU!"

Part 2
I Can Do This

4
I Can Do This Thing Called Health

Knowing ignorance is strength.
Ignoring knowledge is sickness.

Only when we are sick of our sickness
Shall we cease to be sick.

The sage is not sick but is sick of sickness;
This is the secret to health.

71st Verse of the Tao Te Ching

Change Your Thoughts, Change Your Life

Dr. Wayne Dyer

Talk of sickness and disease is everywhere. World Health Organization (WHO), did a study at the turn of the century on healthcare systems throughout the world. The U.S. healthcare system ranked 37 among the world's nations in health. In another study that WHO conducted years later, the U.S. ranked 24th in life expectancy. How is it possible for a wealthy, educated country to have such low ratings? What are we doing wrong? For one thing, too many of our people spend all their time and money trying to look good while underneath it all, they feel terrible.

Typically, poor health is associated with poverty and ignorance, not having essential resources: clean water, healthful food, a good health care system, education. For the most part, people in the U.S. have access to those things, yet many are overweight and experiencing ill health. Why?

It seems we have lost touch with what health really is and how valuable it is to have a healthy mind and body. We have forgotten that health is really about how we think and what we believe.

The Mind Body Connection

If we don't take care of our bodies, take care of ourselves, there are consequences——ill-health, disease, pain, and suffering. If we take care of

43

our bodies, take care of ourselves, there are consequences: We experience health, a sense of well-being, strength, power, energy, youthfulness, vitality. It's a choice that we must make all the time.

Our thoughts, emotions, beliefs, and resolved and unresolved issues, make up our consciousness. Those things we face that we don't know what to do with are part of our consciousness, which, makes up a mental mold, so to speak: If we complain about problems with our body and put all of our focus and attention on what's wrong, we create more physical problems.

Our consciousness is creative. Spirit is creative. IT reads the picture we have in our minds of our bodies, our health and ourselves and goes to work to reflect that picture in our physical bodies and experiences. IT brings the physical into alignment with our thoughts and beliefs. If we believe we are sick, weak, or unhappy, IT goes to work and makes it so. Whatever we feel strongly about, IT creates. IT takes the impress of our consciousness—the good, the bad, the ugly, and the beautiful—and creates something tangible and physical out of it. Spirit does not judge. IT assumes that all is good because IT can only know ITself, which is all Good.

If we are holding a grudge or are resentful of something or someone and are still carrying it whether it is currently going on or happened long ago, we have some deep hurt we have buried and not faced. Whether we are conscious or unconscious of this, the power of our being in that consciousness will demonstrate outwardly whatever is going on inside of us.

Our bodies hold all of our emotions. Our consciousness is not just what we are thinking in our heads. It is contained at all times in every cell of our body. The sooner we can come to peace about what is wrong, forgive ourselves and each other and resolve the conflict, the sooner our bodies can be established in balance, harmony, peace, and joy.

If people really knew they were perpetuating the very thing they don't want by telling everyone and anyone who will listen about how bad they feel, or what is going wrong, they would stop. If they had a better idea about themselves and life, they would think again.

Our Natural State of Being

Health, wholeness, energy, vitality, balance, well-being are our natural state. It is natural for our bodies to be healthy. It is unnatural for them to be sick. It seems we have it backwards. Infinite Intelligence, God, Spirit, Life designed our bodies perfectly. They are made of divine stuff. If given half a chance, they know how to heal and restore themselves to health and balance. They are hardwired to make sure they know how to do everything possible for our survival.

Our bodies are here to serve us, to serve our spirits. We have to be healthy in order for that to happen. Disease is not natural. It is not a part of Life's design. These bodies are beautiful. They are a wonder. They are good. They flourish when they are supported with a greater consciousness of health. These bodies are not evil, but they can be used in ways that diminish our health and well-being, as well as for good.

Affirm what you want to feel, not what you are feeling. If you wake up sick, proclaim your health. Your strength, your energy, and the goodness you want to experience will come alive in you because you have paid attention to it and put your focus on it. It was always there. You activated it. That's how you can use the Power for Good for your health or any other thing.

You Are Not Your Body

You are not your body. That comes as a surprise to some. We get so caught up in living life and doing what we are doing, we forget that we are something so much more. You are not your mind. You are the thinker behind your mind. You are spirit. Spirit lives forever, the mind and body do not. Mind, body and spirit all work together. They are all aspects of us, here on the physical plane.

If you think you are your body, you will come up short at one point or another, worried and concerned about getting hurt, being tired, getting sick, and growing old. It's easy to get depressed if you think you are your body, because sooner or later, the body deteriorates when we come from that place, especially when that is our focus.

If we don't have a better idea for ourselves about our bodies, they will grow tired and old just as so many are doing. If we have a greater idea about who we are and the relationship we have with our bodies and all that is possible, they can serve us beautifully much longer than we ever expected.

First Cause to Our Experience

As the thinker behind the body or the spirit, we have the power to create our experience. Whether we like it or not, we have been playing our part in the creation of our health all along. We have played our part in the creation of our current state of health. The facts are what they are no matter how hard they may be to face. Our thoughts and beliefs play out into our bodies.

When we believe what the world says, that our average life expectancy is whatever it currently is, (I say that because it continues to increase), we consciously or unconsciously find a way to fulfill that time frame. We continue to grow old because we think that is the way of life.

The Reality of Life is that we can have it any way we choose. Why would we choose anything but vibrant health and well-being for our bodies, as this is our natural state of being?

Change Your Thoughts, Change Your Body

We have the power to change our bodies. If they are out of alignment with our true nature, they can be brought back into alignment. Once again or maybe for the very first time, we can experience strong, energetic, vibrant, healthy bodies.

Bodies respond to our mental atmosphere, the collection of our thoughts, belief system, and consciousness. If you don't like the results you are experiencing you need to change your thoughts. If you don't like what you are experiencing in your body, change your thoughts about it. Change your thoughts, change your body. Change your thoughts, change your experience.

As we think more and more positively about our lives and this beautiful Life we are all part of, our bodies respond with more health. They naturally pick up on what is going on with us and move into alignment with all the loving, positive energy. They can't help themselves. It's automatic. Our bodies are a mirror or reflection of us and what is going on inside. You look and feel as good as you do because of all the healthy attitudes and ways of thinking you already have. Keep on going. You are doing great.

Sickness and Disease are Not Life's Design

We do not randomly catch bugs or illnesses or whatever else happens to be "going around." If we did, everyone would get whatever it is and everyone does not. The only way we catch things is if we believe we can or have let ourselves go by not taking care of ourselves. If we are run down, we will be more vulnerable to what is happening around us.

God, or Spirit, doesn't give us sickness or disease as punishment or so that we can learn a lesson. God does not operate that way. How can a God of Love impose pain and suffering on its own flesh and blood. That is not the way of God or the way of Life. IT wouldn't do that. IT can't do that. IT can't go against IT's nature. It is we who have forgotten who we are as spiritual beings. We have separated our own selves from God or Life.

Having said that, there are still going to be times when we don't feel physically healthy. Maybe you are currently experiencing a challenge in this very area of your life or know of someone else who is in that situation. It happens. No need to beat ourselves up about it. We are all merely trying to figure out how Life really works. If you do find yourself there, you must make the best of it and learn all you can from it so that you never have to experience that again.

Great gifts will come out of it if you are open to them. They were there all along, you just couldn't see them. Maybe you weren't open to them or ready for them. Now you are. Infinite Intelligence makes good of everything. You must make good of it all as well.

We never have to get sick to learn. There are plenty of examples around us, stories of people going through difficult health issues, horrible conditions, finding their way. We don't have to learn that way. There are more fun ways to learn.

Our Bodies are Intelligent

My husband and I attended Lamaze classes before delivering our son Joseph. I had been to classes twice before with each of my older children. I never got to really use much of what I learned from them because each of them came early. I still believe in being prepared. I knew I needed a refresher and John, being a first-time father and not knowing what to expect, needed some advice.

In class, the teacher told the average time for labor and said for each consecutive child that time would be cut in half. I said, my first one was 12 hours, my second was in five. Could I really expect to have a baby in two and a half hours? She asked me how long it had been since I had a baby. I said, "Sixteen years." She said, "Oh your body will have forgotten. For you it will be like starting over."

John nudged me and said, "Well that doesn't have to be your truth." And I said, "You are right. Of course, my body will remember." That's not really something a mother totally forgets. I thought to myself, "I bet my body will remember too!"

It did. We had a little joke going as time got closer. One of us would start the morning with "Today is the Day!" When the real day finally arrived I woke up at 5:00 am. with contractions. I met John in the kitchen and all I could get out was "Today is the Day!" He saw that I was in pain and knew this was really it. He timed the contractions and we were off to the hospital. It all happened so fast.

In less than three hours, Joseph arrived. We barely made it to the hospital. Having been stopped by a freight train, we were forced to turn around and go another way. Excited about the prospect of a quick labor, I forgot that the body has to perform the same functions and go through its process no matter how much time it takes. Shorter time meant stronger contractions. Stronger contractions meant more pain all at once. The intensity factor was not considered. For the third time, my bags had not been packed in time.

Intelligence in Action

Before we went to bed one night, my son woke up crying and said that his throat was burning. My mind raced to earlier that day when he had a mad moment on the beach (too much sun?) and shoved a handful of sand in his mouth. Could it be there was something in the sand? He acted so irrational. Maybe he was dreaming. He begged for more and more water and there was no relief. We found a flashlight and looked to see if there was any visible evidence of something wrong.

We decided to do a mind treatment. John treated that we would know what we needed to know about this and have guidance on what to do about it. Just as he finished, Joseph said he tasted acid (acid indigestion). John asked if we had any milk. Thank God there was some milk! I got it from the refrigerator and we gave him some.

It was instant relief! We all were amazed at the chain of events that led to the solution. What a powerful experience we had together! Something inside of us always knows what to do. We just have to access it and listen to the wisdom waiting to be revealed.

Practice Makes Perfect

Joseph's first few years gave us plenty of chances to practice. I wish I could say I've learned everything there was to learn. Several years ago, we were in for an exam and his pediatrician looked in his ears and said they didn't look good. I thought maybe he had an ear infection because he had been playing with his ears. He wasn't complaining. It was good to get confirmation.

Even so, it didn't seem to bother him too much. He didn't have a temperature and he wasn't losing sleep so I asked, "Do we have to put him on an antibiotic? I don't want to have him take medicine unnecessarily." She said, "No" and acted surprised. I said, "The body should be able to take care of this itself, right?" She said, "Yes." Then she went on to say that most parents want her to give their children drugs.

I am sure it assures parents that something is being done about the matter and that they are doing their job as a good parent and that the condition will be taken care.

Most of us have become so dependent on medicine that we don't believe there is any other way to heal. We have forgotten what we once commonly knew, that the body is a million-year-old healer. It knows what it is doing. We wouldn't be here today if it didn't.

Typically, when our children are sick, we panic. Everyone loses some sleep and that isn't good. Results are required to get everyone back on schedule. I just got to a point where I wanted to stop reacting and begin experimenting. Since then, I haven't reacted. I started remembering that I don't have to get all caught up in the condition. I can remember my son's spiritual truth that he has his own divine pattern of perfection and it is up to me to recognize it and call it forth. I am always learning.

We accept way too much of what comes along and think that is what must be, and we pay a price for that. What doctors say is not the gospel truth. We are not trapped in the medical model. We thank God for it because it is good and has saved many lives and we need to remember we use it by choice. We determine our experience of it or decide on an alternative. It is not meant to be the end all. There will always be physical conditions that come up that have no cure. There will always be medicines that don't work. Why? They are all here only to support us with our own program of health.

Heal From Within

I saw a commercial where people were raving about this bracelet that is supposed to relieve you of your pain. You have probably seen them too. They have been around for a long time. People who were interviewed said they were relieved of their pain and feeling young and vital again. Even though it was just a commercial, it was great to see them so alive. Anything and everything that gives us more life is good.

And yet, is that the answer? Can we really stop there? What happens when we lose the bracelet? What happens when we are on vacation and we are in a place where we can't readily get a hold of another one? Does the pain return? Is the vacation ruined? Are we miserable again? If that is true, then the solution doesn't take us as far as we need for it to take us, does it?

What we forget is that we are the power in our life. We don't have to invoke the power of God because it is already here within us and around us. We don't have to beg or plead for it. It's already here. That means we were created to be our own spiritual authority. I know that is blasphemous to some. It's really the only way. You have to do that for yourself. We are here to decide, to choose, to act. Our experience depends on that. We are making decisions and choices and acting, whether we are conscious of it or not, so we may as well do it from a place of personal power.

In 1968, Dr. Raymond Charles Barker wrote in his book *The Power of Decision*,

> *Health is not the body. It is a state of consciousness that permeates the body, but it is not the body. The body can neither make itself ill or well. The body is an impersonal, organized field of substance with no identity of its own. It has no conscious consciousness, so it doesn't know when it is sick or when it is well. It acts out what your consciousness is.*

Okay, what does that mean? It means you guide the body's ultimate fate with whatever patterns of belief you impose on it. You may believe you are thinking positive thoughts about your body and still have physical problems. What do you really believe about your body? What are the habits of thought you carry from your past? What thoughts have you lived with and accepted all your life? Approximately 90% of your mind is your subconscious. That's a lot of consciousness you are not aware of.

Is it possible to change habits of thought that we grew up with and have had all our lives? Yes. It's like cleaning out a basement or a garage that has not been cleaned out in decades. You just have to begin somewhere and start cleaning up.

It's All Good, It's All God

Five years ago, my good friend Carol was finishing her radiation treatments for breast cancer. She did a great job even though it was the most difficult thing she had ever experienced in her life. The treatment program was very aggressive. I believe that what cancer patients go through is a case of overkill. The medical profession has proven that for younger women, chemotherapy and radiation do the trick, once and for all. That gives everyone peace of mind. That is good.

Before any of the treatments started, I said, "I will ask you this once because I have to. After that, I will support your decision to do it the way you think you have to do it. Are you sure this is the direction you want to go with this?" She said, "Yes. I don't have enough belief at this time to take care of it any other way." My experience with her told me that she really had more belief than she thought she had. I respected her belief about where she was and what she needed, and I knew that it is normal to feel less than confident when faced with something we haven't experienced before, especially something as serious as this.

When she was frustrated and wanted to know when it was going to be over, I reminded her that we have to believe the cancer is already gone. We have to focus on health. God is health and health is her natural state of being. I wanted her to remember that she was the power in her life. She was not a victim. She was the one who decided to go through with this whole thing, in this way. We forget that. We need to be reminded that we have made choices. We've made decisions. At any time, we can change our minds, choose again and make different choices. I believe that helped her keep on track. The experience deepened her relationship with Spirit and her faith in ways we would not have guessed. It was an amazing process to watch.

Today, we have become very dependent on the medical profession to help us with our bodies. It's easy to give them all of our power instead of listening to our own bodies and making decisions from our own place of authority. Most of us don't start out with the kind of faith we will need to heal without getting help. We need to be open to all the different forms of help available to us and choose from there. It's all God.

It's important to ask doctors for explanations and opinions, and it's important for us to know that ultimately, we need to decide to do what we can live with, what we can believe in, what suits us best at the time. We need to learn how our bodies work so that we can better work with them and support them.

Our Bodies Listen

My body has been a wonderful teacher. Having baby #3 at the age of 43 proved to be a challenge I would not have guessed. I never had a problem getting pregnant; but I had three miscarriages before our son Joseph arrived. Though my body was still fit, I certainly wasn't 20 anymore.

I had also accumulated some fears I was not aware of when I was twenty. Abstaining from alcohol and drugs was a given; but what about drinking soda with all of its chemicals? I still enjoyed my once-a-week diet coke. What about preservatives and hormones in our food? What about sweets? What about using hair dye? What effect would all this have on my baby? With my greater awareness, these fears played on me.

I added some other things to the mix that weren't there before. Since I had some success with demonstrating what I wanted, could I plan to have a child born during a certain month, making them a certain sign? Silly, I know. As if I even knew what kind of child would be best for our family or who would benefit most from us. Talk about controlling and lack of trust! Living from the head! Information overload. I was messing in places I didn't belong.

To top it off I kept trying to get pregnant without giving my body a break. Finally, an alternative health practitioner who was also a friend said, "You are going to have to build up your body for this. Don't even try again for awhile. We've got to get you stronger."

I lost a lot of blood with my first miscarriage. It was scary. Miscarriages are natures way of releasing. I later learned that they aren't supposed to kill you. They are a natural part of life. The third one came at a really inconvenient time. We had a major speaker coming to town, Neale Donald Walsch, author of "Conversations with God". There were classes and meetings to hold. Once I knew this pregnancy didn't take, I said to my body, "You definitely need to do what you must do and I want very much for you to get on with it *and* I really need to be here for all these events going on. How can we work together? There has to be a way."

My body responded beautifully. My days were mine to do what needed to do be done and to participate in what I wanted to be a part of. My body chose a couple of nights to do its job releasing. My body was listening to me. I was the chooser of my experience. It could all work out. My body was there to support me. We were a team. I learned so much from that experience.

Loving Kindness Is Required

What do you do when you are with people who only know how to talk doom and gloom? Your job is to love them anyway and know that health is their divine nature. Don't let yourself get immersed in their stuff. You can't afford to let that happen.

A close friend of mine was training to be a hypnotherapist and working at a center where she studied. She was making calls to let people know about an upcoming class to help those who wanted to give up smoking. A man confessed to her that he was very embarrassed. He had heart surgery a few months before and people were making fun of him because he was still smoking. He said, "I really want to quit. I just can't." "Having been a smoker", she said, "I understand."

Judgment, guilt, and shame need to be eliminated from the equation as much as possible. Compassion and love are needed for ourselves and others to help reveal our true wholeness, health, and perfection.

Some people want to blame God for their physical problems. They think God should be able to do something and are resentful when things don't change. In the early 1900's, Emma Curtis Hopkins addressed this tendency in Scientific Mental Practice:

"God is health and God is all there is. We already have the freedom to express health. It is up to us. We always have a choice as to how we think and what we need to do."

It's Never Too Late

How many people have given up on their bodies and are resigned to live with them as they are? How many people live with ailments and find relief in drugs and think that is the only way? How many are out of shape and think they can never lose weight? How many believe that they have tried everything?

We are far too accepting of things as they are, especially our bodies. We have a huge toleration for things not being as we would like them to be. If we do believe that change is possible, we may think we are too far gone and it would take more energy, time, and money than we have to make the necessary changes. What we need to know is that it is never too late. There are no damaged goods.

Some people have given up on their minds. They don't believe they can control their thoughts. They think they have seen and experienced too much to change. Yes, the undisciplined mind can be hard to control. Yet, it will respond to your insistence that it change.

Years ago, my mind was all over the place and difficult to keep on track. One of my shorter careers involved taking a programming language called COBOL. It was very difficult for me to stay focused. Yet, it helped me to think things out in a logical sequence. It was a practice in staying focused. At the time, I thought I was doing it to get a better paying job. Infinite Intelligence had something else in Mind.

It's never too late. You are never too old. You are never too sick. Change your thinking, change your body. Change your mind, change your experience!

There is No Need to Fight

The world believes we have to fight for our health and that there are viruses, bacteria, and diseases that are out to get us. Nothing can be farther from the truth. We aren't here to fight anything. We don't have to worry about "catching" something or "coming down" with something from someone or somewhere else.

If we believe that Life is intelligence and that IT creates us intelligently, then we must believe that health is our natural state of being. Fighting implies another power in the Universe we must contend with and there is no other power than the One. Fighting also implies that we have something to fear. There is nothing to fear. There is only something to know. What we must know is how magnificently these bodies are built, how perfectly they were designed. It is our job to focus on making healthful choices and taking care of ourselves, thinking thoughts that keep us in alignment with our Source. A body that is out of balance, neglected, unappreciated, and/or emotional upset on some level, is susceptible to breaking down.

We must learn to respect our bodies. They are here to support us. We need to celebrate them and all they do for us every day. Our focus must be on loving them and ultimately loving ourselves. If we are right with ourselves, our bodies will be healthy.

There is no cancer or anything else to fight. There is only a greater idea to know about ourselves, our bodies, and Life. There is nothing that can harm us or hurt our essence, ever. The greatness that we are, that God being that we were created to be, knows how to heal any suffering, pain, or disease and transform it into greater love, peace, understanding, and joy. All we have to do is accept our God-given health. This is our truth. Let's give thanks and marvel at how perfectly Life works for us all.

Wholeness Is Our Truth

It's hard not to pay attention to verdicts given us by the medical profession; after all, it is their business to know bodies. It takes a lot of courage and determination to believe something other than what they believe or other than what they have experienced. It takes a lot to turn in the direction of our spiritual truth.

The master teacher, Jesus, gives us some of the best examples of physical healing we have seen throughout the ages. He knew his stuff. "By his works may he be known," and he was. When Jesus stood before a sick person, he believed there was a well person within the sick one, a spiritual body within the unhealthy one he saw. His recognition of well-being brought forth health and wholeness.

He didn't make anything magical happen. He didn't give the person back their health. Their health was always there. It was forgotten. It was waiting to be recognized. It was waiting to be called forth. It was waiting to be appreciated so it could make its presence known. Typically, we give all of our attention to what is not right about us physically, instead of what is.

When we recognize ourselves as Spirit, we see ourselves whole. When we recognize the person before us as Spirit, we are recognizing them for who they really are. They may have forgotten, just as we forget. Mark 10:52, Jesus said to the blind man, "Go your way, your faith has made you whole." Immediately, the man received his sight. Jesus was saying, your faith in this idea of health and wholeness makes you whole. Spiritually you are always whole. Your belief in getting sick, catching something or having something else take you over is really not anyone's truth. This is a whole different way of looking at things. If we give our power to the idea that something else can overpower us then we believe in more than one Power and that cannot be.

It's All About Circulation and Flow

We are part of an amazing Universe. What happens on one level must happen on all levels. That is a universal law. Life is all about circulation, ebb, and flow. The tides come in and out. The seasons change. What goes around comes around. What you put out, you get back.

Our bodies have their own requirements regarding circulation and flow. They need to be active. They love to be exercised and used for good purpose. They require clean water and good food. Bodies have to release what is no longer needed. All of these are a part of keeping them working their best.

Our oldest, Nick, was recently working with a paraplegic who hadn't moved in five years. This young man sold his drums because he saw no further use for them, and hadn't even left his house except when he absolutely had to for medical reasons.

Nick told him he had to get the music—vibration, energy—moving through him again and offered to venture out with him on a small trip. Nick knew that the young man needed to be back in circulation on all levels in order for any kind of healing to take place. You never know how far Life will take you if you don't keep trying. There's no chance of healing if you don't. If you are open to taking the next steps, more will be shown to you as you go. Days later, this young man went to church for the first time in years. He made his debut into the world once again.

The Ultimate Health Program

I will never forget a feisty older woman by the name of Catherine. She was an independent thinker and chose to see chemotherapy as liquid gold running through her veins. She was a metaphysician, which means she believed in the power of her thought and what it could do. She chose to go along with the doctor's recommendations and her own mental work. What a gift she gave me to see chemotherapy in a new way.

Ultimately, our program of health has to be spiritual if it is to be permanent. That's where our real freedom comes. When we discover our spiritual truth regarding our health, we are free. Our truth, spiritually, is that we are healthy and whole. That is how we were created. Whenever and wherever we are set free, we enjoy more life, more energy, more vitality. That's what we really want, isn't it? We want to experience feeling good, which is really more God, more goodness.

The body is not helpless. It doesn't have to fall apart as we go along. It is not susceptible to everything that comes its way. We are not victims. The body does some wonderful things without our awareness, unless we override it with a limited or distorted belief about it and impose that on it.

In an emergency, the body's powerful muscles are called into action at a moments notice. We cut or bruise ourselves and the body goes to work. It knows exactly what to do immediately and begins to repair. The body knows how to convert foods and make them into cells, eliminating whatever it no longer needs. It is a sophisticated creation that allows us to live and enjoy many wonderful activities.

It has been said that every atom of the body is not more than a year old. These bodies are not set in stone, as we once thought. The body we have today is not the same body we had all of our lives. It is constantly undergoing renewal and change.

Gladys, another tough old gal, just turned 102. She had said for years, "My cells are forever replenished according to their original state of perfection." That means we aren't getting copies of copies, like in the movie, *Multiplicity*. We are replacing cells from the original. We get distorted copies as we buy into mistaken paradigms of aging, and they get more and more distorted as we go along.

We have to get rid of these old paradigms, such as believing the body continues to age and fall apart as we go along. It is our belief that makes it so. Not the reality of it. If we believe our bodies are ageless, youthful, and energetic, that's what they will be for us.

There is so much we may not understand about what is happening when we are sick. Many times it is the body re-establishing balance and health. We just have to let it do its thing. It is important not to be too quick to judge ourselves and others about what is going on, and call it bad. We need to be as loving as we possibly can. There is so much to learn.

We are vibrational beings. If we are to support ourselves in maintaining health and balance, we must keep the circulation of the best possible ideas, most loving thoughts, inspirations, visions of what is possible, flowing through our minds and hearts. A healthy self-image is a must.

A healthy body is a sign of a healthy mind.

A healthy mind is a sign of a thinker who knows him or herself and is in charge.

A healthy body is an outward demonstration of a peaceful, harmonious mind.

Body, mind and spirit all work together. When you have all that going in unison, you have a most beautiful thing. One of the most important things we do here is to get all of that working. When we do, we are really cooking! Watch out world!

The most long-lasting, youthful, vibrant, energetic, attractive, beautiful bodies belong to loving, supportive, youthful-thinking, vibrant, energetic, beautiful spirits. If you want to be attractive your whole life long, that is where it begins: inside of you. See yourself for who you really are and enjoy being a light in this world for all to embrace for as long as you live. It is the only way.

I Can Do This Thing Called Health—and So Can YOU!

Something inside of us knows how. It's time to free ourselves with a greater truth and know that we are one with an Infinite Power that knows how to make it so.

Ten Steps to a Long and Healthy Life

Make sure you to do some kind of spiritual practice daily. Whatever it may be, it is invaluable.

Practice appreciation. Give thanks for your body, for your health.

Practice forgiveness, especially with yourself.

Release your mental and emotional garbage, anything that has a negative charge to it.

Eat well, drink lots of water, and exercise a minimum of five or six (best of all) times a week.

Be creative in all you do; be generous with your time, talent, and treasure.

Hang out with positive people who encourage and uplift you, who love and support you no matter what.

"Getaways" are always good. They give you a new perspective.

Praise life and everything good.

Most of all, Love Yourself!

Mind Treatment: Perfect Health and Wholeness

Step 1

Infinite, Universal Mind, Infinite Intelligence, Spirit is all there is. IT is the only Power and Presence there can be.

Step 2

IT created me as a perfect, beautiful expression of ITself.

I am IT as me. I am Spirit.

Step 3

I enjoy my healthy body. Health and wholeness are my divine nature. My body is made of intelligence that responds to my beliefs about it.

There is a perfect pattern of health and well-being in Divine Mind.

I am perfect health. I am whole. I am strong.

I vibrate with the energy of Life.

I enjoy a clear, brilliant mind and a strong, healthy body.

All of my organs, cells and muscles work perfectly. Every inch of me is made of divine substance. Health is natural. It is my birthright.

I use my body wisely.

I know how to take care of myself.

I make healthy choices.

Step 4

I release any thoughts, beliefs or conditions that reflect ill-health or disease. These are not my truth.

Step 5

I demonstrate strength, energy, agility, and vibrant health in my physical body.

Step 6

I am so grateful for the abundance of health, balance, harmony, and well-being. I am supported by a body that supports me in doing what I love. I love my flexibility, mobility, freedom of movement, and youthfulness. My body supports me perfectly.

Thank you, Spirit, for everything. Thank you for being present with me each and every moment of the day.

Step 7

I wholeheartedly accept all this and more, now and forever.

And so it is!

5
I Can Do This Thing Called Love

If we look at love long enough, we shall become lovely, for this is the way of love. God is Love. If we gaze longingly at joy, it will make its home with us, and we shall enters its portals and be happy.

Ernest Holmes
Science of Mind

Love…where do we start? The word has different meanings for each one of us, depending on our experience with it. We use the word love as if we understand what it means. Yet, do we really understand the power of love that is continuously operating in us, and what it can do through us and around us at all times? Do we really see and appreciate all the love and support there is for us? Is it possible for us to really love ourselves?

Everyone is at a different place with this and it is perfectly fine to be wherever you are. No need to worry or be concerned if you feel as though you don't know what you are doing when it comes to love. There are plenty of opportunities around us every day to learn more about it. In fact, I believe that is the reason for our being here: to expand our experience of love, enjoy it thoroughly, and give it back to the world in even greater ways. We are here to learn all we can about it, master it, and finally, become the exemplification of love.

We are beings of love. We have a great desire to become great lovers to the world, and to have a greater appreciation and awareness of what is possible for us all. This chapter helps us do that, by covering two aspects of love: Love Relationships and Love as a Way of Life.

Love Relationships

Every human being, and possibly everything in existence, has the capacity to enjoy an abundance of loving relationships. We enjoy Loving Others: family, friends, neighbors, and sometimes even people we barely know. We enjoy Loving Ourselves, and at some point in our lives, most of us enjoy at least one Romantic Relationship.

Loving Others

One day a few years ago, my daughter Liz called on the phone. The first words out of her mouth were, "Mom! Can you go to your computer right away?" I was cooking dinner, and immediately turned off the burner. What could this be? I had never had such an urgent request from my daughter.

I turned on my computer and followed her directions to YouTube, where with great surprise I watched a video of my daughter. It showed Liz getting her beautiful hair cut and donating it to Locks of Love—an organization that makes wigs for children who lose their hair due to an illness such as cancer. As I watched, I cried, because I know how much her hair means to her.

Liz gave this gift with love. It will live on for children in need for a long time, and she will hold it in her heart always. Others have participated in the experience, too: At the time, the video received 42,369 views.

Whenever we act with great love, follow our passions, follow ideas that come to us that have a strong energy about them, whenever it is our intention to serve others and include all, we give ourselves and those in our world, a gift that lives on. Love truly is a beautiful thing.

We miss the boat entirely if we think for even a minute that we don't need love or that we would be happy without it. It really is more than just a sentiment. Love is natural. We were created out of love. "Love makes the world go round." Love is the glue that holds everything together.

We may think that it hurts to love or that we have been wronged by love. Our mistake is in what we believe love to be. Our mistake is in thinking that what we experienced was love. So many times, it was not. We have so much more love to experience. I am not sure we are at a place where we can accept all the love that is available to us. You can't really say enough about the wonders of love. Nothing we can say or do or make is all it can be without love as our real motivation. Leo Buscalia wrote:

We are not evil, inadequate or incompetent when our relationships fail. It may have been that we were simply overconfident about them, not adequately prepared for them or unrealistic in our expectations of them. Not all relationships are right. As long as values change, insights expand, human facades remain impenetrable and human behaviors unpredictable, we will make mistakes.

Love Is All There Is

We are never alone. Isn't that comforting? It makes me feel better. I don't mean that I mind being alone. I enjoy lots of alone time. I mean being in my life alone, facing whatever I have to deal with...alone. At times, it may feel as though that were true. It can never be. It's not even possible. We can never be disconnected from Life.

Years ago, people stayed in one place. We lived close to our families. Many times we lived under the same roof. There were people there for us. Generations lived in the same neighborhoods for decades. Today, that has changed for many people. Job positions have taken many a long way from home. The downside is that many people miss being close, feeling like they are a part of family. We can't always be there for each other. While the quality of our lives has vastly improved by outward appearances, the emotional support of families and friends has suffered. It isn't always easy to start over and make new friends, find your place in a community. There is a loss of connection. It's easy to feel lonely.

Does that mean that we go back to the way things used to be? No. There is never going back. Life is about change. The upside to living away is being independent, making decisions that are right for you, and living the life style you want to live. Things are not like they were yesterday and they aren't suppose to be. Opportunities have taken us far from home. We were meant to branch out, to find ourselves. We were meant to grow and expand our horizons.

Today, more is required of us than ever before to even get on the playing field of life. It requires us to study, to keep up, to get help, to be coached, to practice. We can no longer "wing it" and expect to succeed. We must learn tools and skills to better support us so we can participate in the world in more meaningful ways.

Life on planet Earth has become very sophisticated. After all, we are evolving. So we know more, we are aware of more and more is expected. We expect more of ourselves *and*...it is clear we cannot do life all by ourselves. (as if that were even really possible) The day of the lone ranger is gone. We need mentors. Getting help is nothing to be ashamed about. We need good examples to follow. We can't possibly know it all. We need each other.

There is a point in our development where we must do things for ourselves. A young child will say, "I can do that," "I can do that myself." That's good. It's healthy and there are things we can only do for ourselves. We also have to be able to see our limitations and admit that we need help. And there is no reason why we shouldn't always have a "Life Support Team" available to us.

Life Support

If you were having a medical problem, you would expect to get life support. Why not expect to have life support in other ways? Too many people are having a difficult time keeping up with the current changes, hardly surviving, insisting that things stay the same, fearing the unknown, thinking and feeling that the world is falling apart, not having the tools needed to survive in today's world. I am not saying we have to consult with someone about our every move. But sometimes we can do more by ourselves by just knowing people are there for us if we need them or that just a phone call or email away, we have people who believe in us out there in the world.

If you belong to a community that shares universal life principles and you are part of a group of loving, supportive, like-minded people, you are very fortunate. It is a rare and beautiful thing.

We all need people we can call upon, to listen to us, to love and accept us for who we are, to know what potential is there for us. A higher order of being will always tell us what we need to know in the most loving way. Looking back on my life, there has always been that higher order of being there for me, people I knew I could call to support me in making the tough decisions I needed to make for myself. Sometimes family can't help us with that. They are too close to the situation. They know us as we once were. What we are attempting to do is too close to home for them. Talking about it might mean they would have to face something themselves as well.

Even as I moved around the country during the hardest and most horrible of times, there was always someone there to walk me through it, even if all they knew to do was lovingly listen. They were all beautiful beings with whom I felt comfortable and safe to be myself.

I remember during one particularly difficult period I was going through, my mother, my closest friend, and my daughter would all check in about the same time. Each of them, unknowingly, would call the same day. On some level, they knew something was up with me even when I couldn't always talk about it. It was comforting to know they were there, leaving me a message, loving me. I noticed and was grateful. It helped me to see how loved and supported I was.

I believe someone is always there for us all...even when it doesn't appear to be that way, there is, because that is the way Life works. Life is always present for us to the degree that we are open and receptive to it. Life wants to be support us more and more when we are ready for that. Isn't that great to know?

Here's an example of what I mean that really touched me. I was shocked, along with many others, to hear about the death of Steve Irwin, the Crocodile Hunter, who was dedicated to bringing wildlife into the hearts of people through his TV shows. Shortly after his death, his daughter Bindy was working on her own show, and the reporter was questioning whether it was too soon for her to be doing this after her father's death.

I thought about it for a moment and disagreed. Yes, it is essential to grieve, and it is heartbreaking for a young girl to lose her father. Yet, she picked up his cause and accepted her role, and was continuing what they both loved doing together. She was surrounded by family and friends whose lives were centered around wildlife. It was her life. What a support that was for her, and how could she not stay connected and feel close to her father through it all as she carried on his legacy? How beautiful is that? There is no way she can or should forget him. His presence is all around her. He is a part of her and she a part of him. The pain was converted.

She is a cute little girl and I saw our son, Joseph, then nine years old, watching the segment when I came into our living room. When I asked him at breakfast what he thought of her, he smiled and said, "She's cute." Then he added, "I would like to be with someone like that when I get married." I asked, "why?" He said, "Because she's involved in something interesting." It made me smile to see that he is already on a much higher track in his thinking about relationships, especially a close one like marriage. Many of us had sex, married and procreated with less information. He is already working on his own Life Support Team. Yes!

We need each other. We need to be surrounded by people we can count on. We are all interconnected. We are all really one. We need people who know us, love us, and accept us for who we are. We need to be courageous enough to attract people who will give us honest feedback and tell us the hard to hear things that we must face in order to move forward. We need to know people who aren't scared off easily by the conditions of our lives, and that usually means individuals with large hearts and very open minds.

Imagine your own Life Support Team. What would that look like? What would that feel like? Once you can see it in your mind, it will begin to appear. When you are ready, it will show up. It is more than likely already in place, ready to move into position. All you have to do is believe it exists and say "yes" to it coming into your life.

Ralph Waldo Emerson wrote,

I do not wish to treat friendships daintily, but with the roughest courage. When they are real, they are not glass threads or frostwork, but the solidest thing we know.

Attracting Healthy, Supportive Relationships

Sometimes we don't feel so supported. Those around us either do not know how, or do not have a willingness, to give in a more loving, supportive way. They may not be healthy enough mind, body and spirit to have a clue. It is important for us to know we are supported and loved. It's a basic need. It's important for us to have a better idea of what is possible in order for us to attract healthier, more wholesome relationships into our lives. Healthy, balanced individuals do exist and here's what they look like:

Healthy, loving people love themselves.

They see themselves as a work in progress, green and growing.

Working on bettering themselves is their practice.

They are committed to being all they can be, and start each day with the intention of living better than the day before, which includes bringing something fresh and alive to their relationships.

They tell the truth and have the courage to bring up the "difficult to have" conversations with those they love.

They feel secure in themselves, and know they can move beyond any hurt or pain.

They take themselves lightly.

They intend to resolve conflict.

They agree to disagree with their loved ones, knowing everyone has their own perspective and opinion.

They know themselves, faults and all.

They love themselves and those they are involved with unconditionally.

They see everyone as a part of the human family and support them wherever they can.

They take responsibility for their own happiness.

They practice their spirituality in order that they may deepen and expand their relationship with their highest self and the God of all Creation.

They continue to grow and their relationships grow too.

As we embrace healthy, wholesome, and loving qualities, characteristics, and behaviors, and incorporate them into our own lives, we will naturally and easily attract people who exemplify them as well. These are the kinds of people who can really be available to support us. These are the kinds of people we want to surround ourselves with. They truly are a gift.

Loving Ourselves

Sometimes it's easier to love others than to love ourselves. Loving ourselves may be one of the most difficult things to learn. Sometimes it seems as if no one loves or understands. We feel alone, as if we are in this thing called life all alone. When this happens, we find ourselves in that place where it seems there is nothing we can do to change how we feel. It seems there is nothing we can do to attract more love. We tend to think love is about what we receive from others, and we do all kinds of things to get people to love us. In our failure to understand love, we get stuck.

What *is* the nature of Love and how do we enjoy more love in our lives? The nature of love is that it is all powerful, all knowing and everywhere equally present. God is love and God is everywhere equally present. That means that at every point of existence, God is present in IT's entirety. That means right where you are, God is present. Right where you are, love is already there. At any given moment, we are all immersed in the presence of a higher power. It doesn't matter what you call IT. This also means that you are always surrounded by, and immersed in love. That is the nature of Life and Love.

Why are there times we can't see it or feel it? Because we are out of alignment with love or whatever else is our good; we don't believe that it already exists for us and is available to us. We just need a better idea. We are always loved and supported whether we are aware of it or not. When we recognize love and its power, we begin to consciously use it in our own lives.

Our desire for love, our yearning for it, is really a desire that comes through us to give love. Our aching hearts are really a signal that we are out of alignment with our Source. We are out of alignment with Life's design. We were never meant to live a loveless life. We were never meant to be all alone. We were meant to interact and share life's experiences with love. Amazing things happen when we come together in love. We create an opening for Spirit to work with us.

The ache we feel is always a signal for us to initiate more love, to activate it in our own lives. Love comes forth in us as we come to recognize that it is there. As we remember more and more that it is already ours, we see that it has always been there for us and always will be. We wouldn't be alive without it. We begin to love ourselves and others more, and spend less and less time and energy trying to get something we already have.

Spirit is our source of love. Being one with the Infinite means we have an endless supply at our disposal at all times. We are all channels for that love. That means you and I are channels for our own love. We begin by being more loving to ourselves. How we love and take care of ourselves determines how well we love and care for others, so this is a very important place to start.

When we activate love within us by giving it to ourselves and those around us, it grows, it heals, it transforms. As we increase our capacity to give, we create an opening for more love to flow back to us. This means we have even more to give than ever. That process goes on indefinitely because we are infinite beings. Life is incremental. IT is about growth. IT will do everything IT can to support us and reward us as we stretch, grow, and expand because we are a part of Life forever unfoldi through each and every one of us.

We must learn to love ourselves before we can truly love someone else. That may seem like an impossible task. There will be those who resist this idea and insist on finding someone else to love them. They say, "I can't love myself" and fully expect someone else to, even though they can't. That is a red flag there. They will find someone to love them, or at least give them what they think love is. But because it is coming from the outside, it will never be enough. It won't be long before they doubt that person's love. Discouraged, disappointed, they then look for someone else to fit the bill. No wonder so many are disillusioned with love.

The world doesn't help matters. It teaches us how to be cool, how to dress, what to say, what to do. Wear this to be popular or attractive sexually. From childhood on, we are programmed by TV, ads, and commercials to believe we need a certain product or look in order to be acceptable and fit in. We learn a lot about all the externals, and very little about character or values.

Finding love is never about being in the right place at the right time. It is always about being the right person all the time. When we know love is already inside us, that we are loving beings to begin with, we aren't concerned about where our love will come from. When you know that you are a spiritual being, you don't have to worry about being good enough. You don't have to have money. You don't have to be young. You don't even have to be beautiful. Beauty comes from within, and can't be faked. If you are happy with who you are, you will always be enough right here and now.

We never have to wait for someone else to love us in order to experience love. We don't have to wait for the "right one" to show up before we "fall in love". We don't fall in love just because the right person shows up. We fall in love when we realize who we are, that we are an expression of the Infinite, created perfectly out of ITs great love, here to have an amazing experience.

We can't save our love or hold back from giving it until we have that special one in our lives. If you want a life filled with love, you must spread it everywhere you go, to whomever you meet: to the clerk at the checkout counter, or the person bagging your groceries, complimenting them, encouraging them. Give love to a difficult situation, your bills, your past, whatever you are dealing with. Give as much as you can under any and all circumstances. Become a direct channel for love to the world, starting with yourself. Treat yourself well. Give love freely and easily and you will always have an abundance of it. You will feel that you are floating on air. Get that belief going in your life and you will always be happy. You will never be without love again.

There is no saving the love we have for someone else to come along, because we already have that special person in our lives: us. You are the only person who can never leave you. You have a lifetime to get to know yourself and see what you can do in this wonderful world of form, what you can master, what you can create. Loving ourselves is being able to truly appreciate the beautiful being that we are. This is the very thing that guarantees success in our relationships with others.

The big secret to finding loving relationships is to *be* love. Be a loving partner with yourself first, and next, with the rest of the world. In order to find the "Right One", you have to *be* the "Right One." A person who is a joy to be with has learned to love themselves, mistakes and all. They have an appreciation for who they are and what they have gone through. They are in touch with their real self, not some made-up character. They are genuine and honest. They aren't trying to please the world--as if that were even possible. They please themselves. They are inner-directed. They like who they are. When you love yourself and enjoy your own company, it doesn't matter what does or doesn't happen; you are happy. You always have yourself. Be the person you would like to be with, and you will always have plenty of love in your life.

Romantic Relationships

Millions of people today live alone, some by preference, others not. For some, the single most important thing to get is a love relationship, to have someone to love and someone who loves them back.

So often, we live in a fantasy of having an ideal partner who is perfect in every way. Is that even possible? Hardly. We aren't perfect so how can we expect anyone else to be? Sooner or later, we run into difficulties. The honeymoon period is over and things no longer seem so perfect. The surge of hormones coursing through our veins hides a lot of things. Things we didn't want to see, or missed at first glance, begin to come to the forefront. We begin to wonder what we got ourselves into. This person may not be the answer to our prayers. There are problems. Now we are in a bigger mess than when we were alone. "What have I done?" we ask. Ever happen to you?

There was a bumper sticker that read, "If all the good ones are taken, does that mean I'm not one of the good ones?" Similarly, there's a joke that goes, "If all the good ones are taken, what does that make me…chopped liver?"

Personal Responsibility

When problems arise in a relationship, it's tempting to put the blame on the other person for being a certain way, and for making our life miserable. It was easy to blame my first husband for our problems because of a confession he made. I blamed him for it all. I was angry. I was done. And before our marriage was completely over, I became involved in an extramarital relationship, which only took me from bad to worse. Not a good place to start a new relationship. Because I was in such an unhealthy place, I attracted someone else with serious problems. Help!

One afternoon several years into the second relationship, after my divorce, I entered the beautiful foyer of the office building I worked in, it hit me that I was helping to create the unhealthiness of the relationship. I suddenly understood that the more I talked about, complained about, deliberated about the mess the worse it got, and it had grown to a point that was unbearable. I was participating in evil and keeping it alive.

This awareness stopped me cold in my tracks, and from that moment on, any time I began to go down that old familiar path, I made a conscious effort to stop and affirm "I am in a healthy, loving relationship" because that is what I really wanted to experience. The instant I took my power back in this way, I felt better about myself, and things soon calmed down on the home front. I had changed the dance.

"Dance" is a perfect way to describe how we express in relationships. It takes great effort to change from one dance to another, and it's exactly what's needed to create something better. As one partner changes, the other will also.

That is, unless one partner wants to keep on doing the same old dance; then they have to find a new partner who likes to dance that way. I used to worry about leaving my partner behind. There is no need to worry about what will happen to them if you should leave. There's a line of eligible new recruits just waiting to move into your place.

Several months after taking my power back, I understood my part in creating messy relationships. I realized that it was irresponsible for me to claim "victimhood," because I was responsible for my part in what happened in them. In my marriage, I was so busy with the kids, a large home, and my work in the world that I had nothing to give myself or my husband. As for the affair, it never stood a chance because it was founded on my anger.

Ultimately I realized I was most angry at myself for not taking care of me. Upon moving into my own place, I started the real work I needed to do. For the first time in years I was free to focus on myself. This work would be the transition from one way of living to another. A new chapter in my life began. Fortunately, this difficult time marked the beginning of my spiritual journey and the rebuilding of my life. I launched a search for a better way to think and live. It took several years of seeing therapists, a psychiatrist, and taking classes before I started to pull myself together. It was time. I had been depressed and feeling guilty for much too long. One therapist told me I was close to being committed. That got my attention! I would have none of that.

At that point, I found my spiritual home and started investing time in a spiritual practice that fed me healthy, loving ideas that soon bore fruit.

Time in the Desert

Love is not always an area that I have done well in, at least in the area of romantic relationships. I have always believed in love. I have always loved people and been loved by them. But to be a great lover, we need to love and appreciate ourselves as expressions of Spirit.

By my early 30's, my heart felt raw. I had been through the mill. I was ready to say I had experienced a lifetime of heartbreak. But it was hardly a lifetime, and it wasn't all bad. I was 34 at the time. After a 9-year marriage and another 4-year relationship, I remember saying to my mother, "I need a break from men." A "time out" was definitely in order. A "man-fast" would help me heal. I never admitted that to myself before. Now it was clear.

My cousin invited me to a Center for Spiritual Living, and I can't thank him enough. The teaching is based on a simple truth: "Change your thinking, change your life." This was exactly what I needed. There was hope for me and my life. I could give up feeling like a failure. I could begin again free of the distractions of living with someone else. In the safety and security of this beautiful new way of thinking, as well as being in the company of others who were working on themselves, I was able to get to know myself for the first time as a spiritual being. For the first time, I was learning how to imagine what was possible.

It is best to take time to heal. There is no need to rush into love. Why bring all that garbage into your next relationship when you can start out clean and clear? Better to get things right with yourself. We think we must have a relationship, that we can't possible live alone but we can. Many people today are doing just that and are quite happy. It might be better to give yourself a chance to get to know yourself before you involve someone else in your life. Hindsight is wonderful!

During my time of "wandering in the desert," I visited my brother and his family. They were off doing something else and I stood in their living room. Taking the moment to reflect. I asked myself, "Why haven't you picked nice, settled, family men like your brothers? What really was so attractive about a challenge in your early days?" That was a big turning point for me, a really good realization!

I was in the desert, and I was okay with being there. It felt so good to have no one to answer to except myself, no walking on eggshells about anything. No heartache. It was one of the greatest gifts I have ever given myself. It was the beginning of a whole new way of life.

Cocreating with the Universe

After spending almost two years on my own, without a relationship, I felt better than ever. It felt good to have my strength and confidence back. I was no longer a pushover. I knew what I wanted, or at least I was getting clearer about what that was. I had proved myself to me! I was healthy and happy. I knew I was ready to attract a healthy, wholesome relationship. I had a greater idea of what was possible. I definitely knew what I didn't want. I was ready to see what the next generation of relationships would look like for me. I also recognized this new relationship needed to unfold at a slower, easier pace.

Let me tell you about John...

John was one of my first big demonstrations from doing treatment work, or affirmative prayer. It was a small investment of my time, energy, and focus compared to the final outcome, which still continues to unfold. I was coming from a sincere, genuine, authentic place of heart and a desire to demonstrate a relationship like none I had ever experienced. I had no idea what the Universe could do. What IT did was to bring this guy from Connecticut to Atlanta, where I lived at the time. The Infinite does nice work.

When my new guy didn't show up, I decided to take up tennis. At least I would get more exercise. I worked with married men, my running partner and friend was gay, and I was attending a church with a large gay population at the time. One day it dawned on me that I was not really in circulation. I needed to open up some channels for my good. I knew it was not going to be the pizza delivery guy, so I needed to do something that would expose me to new people.

Shortly after this, I was invited to a Round Robin one Sunday afternoon at a nearby apartment complex. There was John. He was a nice guy, attractive, and we found ourselves talking away after everyone else left. He had just been through some very difficult circumstances and was ready to begin a new life. It wasn't long before he wanted to know all about Science of Mind and spiritual living. Of course, I was happy to share all the exciting concepts I was learning. It wasn't long before he became a significant part of my life and within three years, we were married.

I am reminded of a business trip I took to Oklahoma shortly after re-marrying. My driver was an older cowboy type and we had miles to travel together before reaching our destination. In one of our conversations, he said that he picked his first wife, and God picked his second. I couldn't help but smile. I, too, had picked my first. In fact, I realized that I had picked all of the men in my life. I had to look at the cold, hard fact that where relationships were concerned, I wasn't so good at picking. They weren't right for me. If there was to be another major relationship in my life, this one was going to have to come to me, and it did. God picked and it made all the difference. I knew exactly what the cowboy was talking about.

Love and Sex

Many people experience difficulties with love and sex. That's because it's not just a matter of two people coming together. We aren't taught much about being in any relationship, especially the relationship with ourselves, which is critical to our success here. Throw sex into the mix and it further complicates things. Sex can make us feel more vulnerable. When we feel vulnerable, our unhealed areas come to the surface. Included in that are all the unhealthy messages we get about our bodies while we are growing up.

Sex, a beautiful physical expression of love and tenderness, is made more difficult in these times by the fear of AIDS and other venereal diseases. Then there's the questions of whom can we trust, and the fear of getting pregnant.

There is a lot to unlearn that doesn't serve us. There is pain to overcome, and a greater consciousness to bring to this area of love and sex. I am here to tell you that no matter what you have experienced, Love with a capital "L" can handle it all and set you in a beautiful new direction. There is a way to bring sanity to all this confusion, so that we can once again enjoy ourselves and our bodies, which were created to be temples of the living God.

Spiritual Marriage

Ralph Waldo Emerson wrote,

The Deity sends the glory of youth before the soul, that it may avail itself of beautiful bodies, as aids, to its recollection of the celestial good and fair; and the man beholding such a person in the female sex runs to her and finds the highest joy in contemplating the form, the movement and intelligence of this person, because it suggests to him the presence of that which indeed is within the beauty, and the cause of the beauty.

In other words, whoever we are, we may be attracted to one another physically, but there is always some greater reason for us being brought together. There is more to physical attraction than the body. That's just one level of experience. There is something more that suggests the inner beauty…and ultimately the cause of that beauty… the Creator… Life… Magnificence ITself, *that* is the real point of attraction.

We come together for reasons beyond what we are aware of. We think we are coming together for the sex, for fun, companionship, shared interests, love, and understanding. These are all good reasons, but Life has something more in mind. IT brings us together so we can learn about each other, come to know ourselves more greatly in our togetherness, get to try on different points of view, and ultimately see the entire human race in each other, stretch in our love. Experience shows us all the things that can surface when we are in a relationship. Together, we get to address them all, provided there are two people who love one another and who both want to grow to accomplish more together. Both need to have a willingness to work problems out. If you don't have that, it's not much of a relationship; it's a never-ending battle.

Emerson continues,

There's a marriage behind and beyond the marriage that is greater than what we can see that happens, that bonds us, that deepens, that matures us and provides us a greater place to love from. We are put in training for a love which goes beyond the couple.

This of course doesn't always happen. More often than not, as we see evidenced around us, it does not. People change their preferences, change their minds, find someone else, are not compatible, grow in different ways and at a different pace. That's going to happen, too, along the way. It's a part of life.

Nevertheless, we can trust that Love will have it's way with us all and that Love will find a way to succeed in us and our lives. We can trust that whatever ground we have gained in our previous relationships will be surpassed in the next. Psychologists used to refer to this as stair-step relationships. We learn from them and we move into a greater love and maturity as we go. We have to be loving with ourselves and each other about all of our relationships. They require the best of us, and even then, they are a continuous practice.

People genuinely are good and want to do right. They want to experience greater success than they have had. As long as we have learned from our past mistakes in relationships, they have served their purpose. The good news is that God is never sitting on the bedposts judging what is going on. God, which can only be Love, lives in the hearts of the people. Love is always there for us.

We must remember that no one is ever harmed by love.

The more love there is in your life, the better off you are.

Love builds up, it doesn't destroy.

We must learn to feel the presence of Love and rely on it.

Love begins with a healthy relationship with ourselves.

If it is loving, if it grows, expands, or deepens love, it's the right thing to do.

LOVE AS A WAY OF LIFE

Love really is all there is. This next section addresses the healing power of love, how the love we give returns to us and the power of our relationship with Spirit. When we recognize the magnificent power of love in our life, love will become a way of life for us. When that happens it is like stepping into a new dimension. It's rich, juicy, and alive. We feel and enjoy love like never before.

We live in a world that worships the intellect. Many of us are very sophisticated thinkers. We have been studying for a long, long time. We can talk about things very well. We can rationalize and analyze with the best of them. Have you noticed that as stimulating as all that may seem, it doesn't necessarily get you what you want? Understanding, intellectually, what we want is not enough to get us the results we seek. Why? Because we've been circling the idea of what we would like to see happen in our life with our thoughts and have not yet embodied them with our feelings. We haven't become one with it. We haven't become the thing we want to experience. We haven't become the love and given the love we want to receive.

We know that when we really want to do something, nothing and no one will get in our way. We may not know the way it can happen, but we are positive that it will happen. We say, "I'm in. You can count on me." Every part of our being says "Yes." It's something we just have to do. It has our name written all over it. We say "Yes" before we even know the details. We are ready!

This is the interesting part: we don't even have to think about it. I felt that way when I started seeing the results of applying universal spiritual principles to the different areas of my life. I was passionate about having a connection to God. There were things happening that I could never have brought into being on my own in a million years. That may be an exaggeration but you get the point. Things started happening that I wanted to share with those around me.

John and I have been on a wonderful journey that continues to unfold, each of us is growing and expanding, becoming more real, each one of us is drawing closer. Who would ever have thought that our first meeting would lead to 20 years together, a beautiful child, and doing the work we love?

But it has happened, because with all my heart, I was "in on it" happening. There have been times when I wanted something to happen that didn't, or that only happened partially or didn't happen at all. I see now that I was tentative. I wasn't fully committed. I hesitated. I was afraid. I wasn't thinking big enough. I forgot who I was and what I could do. Hence, the results were not what they could have been. It was disappointing and discouraging because my heart was not in it, only my head…only part of me.

Wholeheartedly means totally present with our entire being. We are excited and committed to doing whatever it takes. There is an intense feeling that goes beyond what we think. When we are enthusiastic, we are inspired by God. We are connected. We are in touch with what is important to us at the heart level. We are passionate about it. I am passionate about enjoying a healthy body and doing whatever I can to support it, because I know that is a part of loving myself. I know how beautifully my body takes care of me when I treat it well.

When we are enthusiastic about something at the heart level, we are energized; time doesn't exist and we spare no expense.

We are incapable of doing what we want, living the life we want to live, having the experiences we want to have, when we are not wholeheartedly behind ourselves and our life. It is tiring to create from a place where we are half dead, where every part of us is not behind what is happening or what we are trying to do. That kind of life experience sucks us dry and makes us old. We give up for lack of a better idea.

How many times do we say we would like to do something and never put forth the effort it takes to prepare ourselves for it? Then we wonder why it never happens. It hasn't happened because we haven't been behind it with our whole heart and soul. We haven't trusted our heart to carry us forward.

We haven't fully said yes to the idea because we don't think it could happen. Maybe we don't have the funds or resources. Maybe we aren't clear about our intention for doing it. Maybe we think we have to do it all ourselves. Maybe we are too busy and distracted. Maybe we take on too much, so that we are always in a state of pressure and panic, feeling overwhelmed. While this may explain what prevents us from moving forward, it still won't happen unless we change our ideas. Only then can we move forward.

I invite you to join me in letting ourselves get so wrapped up in the idea we want to experience that the enthusiasm, the inspiration of God comes through so strong that it lifts us up to a new level where the creation of a healthier body, loving relationships, work that we love, whatever it is, takes place in the most natural and easy way we have ever seen.

Ask yourself

What am I enthusiastic about?

What would I do if money were not an issue?

What am I wholeheartedly behind?

Those are the areas you have demonstrated well in. Living without them is not an option for you. You just have to do them, and you do. No question about it.

What am I fascinated by, what do I find compelling, thrilling, and awesome?"

With all my heart...I can do great things.

With all my heart...I can do the things I really love.

With all my heart...My life works.

With all my heart...I live the life of my dreams.

With all my heart...others are happy to come on board and be a part of my team...be in my life.

With all my heart...I can accomplish anything.

With all my heart...I fulfill my reason for being.

With all my heart...greater things than these are there for you and me.

John Keats wrote,

I am certain of nothing but the holiness of the Heart's affections and the truth of Imagination – What the imagination seizes as Beauty must be truth – whether it existed before or not.

Living from your heart is huge. It is freeing. It answers questions you didn't know how to answer before. It makes your way known to you.

When you say, "With all my heart, I really want to . . . " nothing or no one, especially you, will get in the way. All the forces of the universe will be right there with you and make it so. You can choose to live from this place right now, today.

Love Heals All

Love is really more than being in a relationship. When things look their worst, it is time to remember love. It all begins with us. Love heals all.

When our son Joseph was little, he attended the Jewish Community Center. We trusted that he would be in good hands there. We weren't sure we could trust the Christian schools because of what they might say regarding the devil and hell, or being saved or having to be reborn in Jesus. Our child would not be exposed to that.

Well, every place has challenges. Especially at this time, right after 911, people were afraid Joseph's school would be a target. One of the mothers actually pulled her child out of the school because she was afraid. It was a decision she made for herself and her child. It was the right thing for her to do. It's not good for the child if the parent is worried.

I did not have that same sense of fear. Both John and I questioned our own child's safety and agreed that we would pull him out if we were guided to do so. We never got that guidance. We had a particular advantage of staying present with all the good that was taking place at the school because we didn't share a Jewish heritage. Sometimes you are just meant to stay and love, be the stabilizing force that holds things together. We felt that was what we were doing.

Love Always Returns

It has taken great love to get us all where we are today. You and I would be nothing without love. We wouldn't even be here very long. It takes courage and love to realize we are a greater being than we first knew ourselves to be. It takes a huge love to figure out why we are here and what we need to do about it.

My teacher once said, "Love always returns to where it started, better for where it's been." I really like that. During the breakdown of my early 30's, I took most of the relationships I had with family, and especially the one I had with my children, to a breaking point. It's one thing to have a divorce. It's another thing to leave your children. At the time, I didn't believe I had any other choice. I needed some time to get myself together and figure out what was going on. I didn't have the kind of work that could support them. I didn't have the strength to face a custody battle, and I loved them too much to have them go through that. Thank God, there were deep reservoirs of love supporting all of us. I felt as though I was all over the map, and quite literally, I was moving from one coast to the next, with smaller moves in between.

No one, especially me, really knew what I was going through. I was on the edge. I doubted myself, so I could fully understand why my family was wondering about me. They did their best. It's tough to break out of a mold, to leave the lifestyle that we have been brought up with, to leave the religion of our families, to reject the old without rejecting our loved ones. My children grew up hearing concern and speculation about me. There were some tense times between us, and the physical distance made it even more difficult.

A beautiful therapist I worked with in Atlanta guided me. She said, "It's good the children are with their natural father. Do whatever you can to keep the relationship with your children going. Stay in contact. Get together as much as possible. Spend time together. Take them places. Spend the money, even if you don't have it. Enjoy your time together." And that is what we did. We made the very best of the time we had, and I tried to always be available by phone. They were not always so receptive. I had to earn their trust again. I had to earn my own trust again. I had to overcome much guilt and shame.

Things were beginning to change directions. Love had returned for me. I earned the right to it.

Years later, we had an opportunity for author Marlo Morgan, speaker and author of *Mutant Message Down Under*, to visit our center in Orlando and stay at our home. We had a great visit. On the way to the airport, I told her about not having my children with me. She said that it was all the way it was supposed to be, that it was a contract we made together before I even came here. "You needed to separate from them so you could find yourself and a new way of living that you could share with them," she said.

What a gift she gave me that day! What a beautiful way of looking at things. It was true. As soon as I decided I was done with my story and ready to begin a new one, and as soon as I had some spiritual support that helped me learn about the Universe and how it really works, I was sharing everything I could with my kids. This life and wisdom was something they had not been getting from their world. Spirit sparked the love that was always there back into our relationship and we flourished together. Before I knew it, my kids were calling me for help with handling difficult situations in their own lives. Today, we are extremely close and we appreciate the fact that we would not be where we are today without all that happened before.

I would not be who I am today without all of the other relationship experiences I had along the way. Today, I can appreciate them all, especially the most difficult ones.

Our Relationship with Spirit

Amazing as our love relationships and what they mean to us can be, ultimately we must be in partnership with our highest self, the great I AM, as us. The I AM of our being. We must have a solid partnership with Spirit, God, our Source that will feed us, inspire us, guide us, direct us, accept us, love us and provide for us always, no matter what.

That relationship is already in place. We don't have to go out in search of it. We just have to see it and immerse ourselves in the realization of IT more and more. We need to know we are hooked up to our Source. It's the only real life support we need. We can't live without this one. There is no real life without it.

Many die not knowing that they have a bigger part to play in their relationship with God, and from not knowing how they can help themselves, their loved ones and others around them. That does not have to happen. We are here to learn what our role is in that grand scheme of things and play it, practice and perfect working together as Spirit. We are here to step into a spiritually mature relationship with the Universe which is ourselves, all others, and beyond.

Ultimately our spiritual journey is one of learning to love and appreciate who we are. Everything else--our health and well-being, our success and wealth, the love from others--is a reflection. It tells us where we are on our journey and what we need to work on.

We are way overdue for a better idea of love. We have gone as far as we can go without a better understanding of love. There is that within us that yearns to experience more and when that desire is unfulfilled, with no possibility of being satisfied, it will lead people to all kinds of crazy, unhealthy obsessions and perversions. Movies and TV programs are filled with them. In real life, people searching for ways to express their desires and urges get into all kinds of trouble because they are thinking too small about the kind of love they can have or give. They haven't expanded to a grander picture of themselves.

We are missing the major ingredient, which is that we are spiritual beings first. We are something much more than we appear to be. There is a greater experience to have. We are right in thinking there is something missing or something more we want to experience. We have forgotten the Source of our desires, our nature, and fulfillment depends on our thinking from a higher place, opening ourselves up to Infinite Possibility and the divine fulfillment of our needs and desires. That is the promise.

As soon as we take the leap, coming at this from a spiritual place instead of just a physical one, things change. We find greater fulfillment and satisfaction. We may not even need some of the things we thought we once had to have. We open the door to an unlimited experience with Spirit as Love when we recognize that Spirit is our Source.

The One that is Love and that created us all has the answers. The solutions are available to us. They are waiting for you and me to get ready for them. We will not be disappointed.

It's time for us all to take our personal power back when it comes to matters of the heart. It's the only way.

The best is yet to come!

The essence of love, while elusive, pervades everything, fires the heart, stimulates the emotions, renews the soul and proclaims the Spirit. Only love knows love and love knows only love. Words cannot express its depths or meaning. A universal sense alone bears witness to the divine fact: God is love and Love is God.

Ernest Holmes
Science of Mind

I Can Do This Thing Called Love -- and so Can YOU!

Mind Treatment: The Power of Love

Step 1:

There is only Love. God is Love and God is all there is. Love is everywhere. Love is powerful.

Step 2:

I am immersed in the presence of Love at all times.

I was created out of IT.

It courses through my veins.

Love is active and alive in me and in every area of my life.

Step 3:

I am always perfectly supported by Love.

Love opens my heart and sets me free.

I was born to give and receive love.

Step 4:

I can never be without love, even when I believe I am.

Step 5:

I am a great lover in the world and the world loves me back.

I am so filled up with love that there is room for nothing else.

Step 6:

I am grateful for all the love I enjoy in my life.

I appreciate that Life sustains me and supports me always.

Step 7:

Love is all there is! And so it is!

6
I Can Do This Thing Called Work

In the story of Sir Galahad, the knights agree to go on a quest, but thinking it would be a disgrace to go forth in a group, each entered the forest, at one point or another, there where they saw it to be thickest, all in those places where they found no way or path. Where there is a way or a path, it's someone else's way. Each knight enters the forest at the most mysterious point and follows his own intuition. What each brings forth is what never before was on land or sea: the fulfillment of his unique potentialities, which are different from anybody else's. All you get on your life way are little clues.

Diane K. Osbon
Reflections on the Art of Living
A Joseph Campbell Companion

It is your duty to demonstrate, and in order to do so successfully, you need to know why you should do so. Why should you demonstrate at all? Because you have to prove the harmony of your being, in your own life. That is why. If there were no need to demonstrate, one might just as well go to bed and stay there or, more simply still, go to the nearest undertaker.

Emmit Fox
The Mental Equivalent

For many, work is something like prison: means being some place they don't want to be for five or six days a week, and doing something they'd rather not do. They think they have to put in time to survive, to make a living.

Others absolutely love what they do. They don't care about money, because they're passionate about their work. It doesn't even feel like work. It feels like play. It engages, stimulates, energizes, and feeds them, not only monetarily, but also mentally, emotionally, and spiritually.

What if we could experience our work that way?

What if we could enjoy ourselves while doing it?

What if we could find deep meaning in what we do and why we do it, even when the current task is unpleasant?

I believe we can, and that when we have the right attitude, we attract work that's fulfilling and satisfying. We know that we are supported with everything we need.

This chapter is designed to enhance the way we look at work and to change our thinking about it. The truth is that no one is condemned to do what they do now for the rest of their days. We were never meant to slave away or resign ourselves to doing what we don't want to do. We were never meant to be bored to tears, wasting our life away.

We can have it all.

A Bigger View of Work

No matter what our job may be, it's an opportunity to give our unique talents and best gifts to the world; to engage with life in meaningful ways; to work out our differences with co-workers; to do our part; to grow and expand who we are. How we work, who we are when we are doing it, and what we bring to it, becomes our practice, and practice makes perfect. Doing the same thing over and over again, we finally get it right.

When viewed in this way, our place of employment offers us an opportunity to keep doing things better, to grow in responsibility, people skills, and expertise. As we invest more of ourselves into each and every situation on the job, our confidence builds and our self-image expands. We enjoy getting to know more about ourselves and what we're capable of.

As we feel better about ourselves, our job seems easier and changes begin to take place around us. Instead of experiencing work as a chore, dreading and resenting it, we use it as a way to become more polished, earn our stripes, and improve our communication skills and ability to work with people. We practice self-mastery as we face situations and conditions that demand our very best. We learn how to co-create, with Infinite Intelligence, with people who want to be right where they are and are happy to be giving of themselves in a healthier, more loving, and more productive environment. We come together to support one another in being our best as we accomplish whatever project or business is before us.

By making a greater contribution on the job, we reap the benefits of being a more proactive, productive player in Life. New positions and opportunities present themselves. We may even have fresh ideas. We may decide to work independently for ourselves. Any number of things can happen.

Working for the Universe

My last big job before entering the ministry was as an instructor teaching customers how to use a software program for a company in midtown Atlanta. At first, it was a struggle for me to work there, as they required my presence in the office 40-50 hours a week. They would have loved it if I had lived there.

What made the job possible for me was that I knew it was only a stop along the way. This became clear during my third year of class work for the ministry, when I realized that I really didn't work for the company. It was just a channel that happened to be the place I showed up until further notice. My real boss was the Universe, and that was whom I would serve.

I started asking every day, "Universe, how can I best serve you today?" and opportunities showed up. In that busy, mechanical, highly detailed setting, people shared personal information about their lives with me on a daily basis.

I was delighted to work for the Universe and not "the man." As I continued to ask the all-important question, "Universe, how can I best serve you today?" Life became enjoyable everywhere I was because I was free. I didn't "need" the company I worked for. I was there temporarily, and I knew Life was taking me other places. In the meantime, I would give them my very best and love the people there as well as I could.

But even this way of looking at work is limited, because work is not just doing a job we're paid to do. It's everything that comes up for us, whether it's specifically job-related or not. Anything and everything that has to do with us is our work and our practice.

The True Meaning of Work

The Universe doesn't care whether we're "at work" or not, whether we have the day off or are on vacation. If we're open to it, some of the best work we do can occur when we're "off." There's downtime. We're free of our schedule and other distractions. The Universe sees this time as an opening, and with no warning, presents us with situations that want to be healed. Suddenly, we find ourselves getting mad about some long-standing disagreement with a family member, or some other source of contention. If we can recognize it as a golden opportunity instead of a bad experience, we can work it out once and for all, compliments of the Universe.

The work we came here to do is to continually unfold. The Universe--Life, Spirit--works us from every angle; not because we're bad or evil, but simply because something better is always trying to happen for us. Spirit wants the very best for ITs own, and we belong to IT.

So what we call work can also be play. Every time something happens that we don't like, we can bless instead of curse it, knowing it has to be good for us and will free us in some way, simply because it's happening. Our work is to embrace it all.

As multi-dimensional beings, it's exciting and engaging to live on more than one level at a time. When we get an "ah-ha" moment, a moment where we realize more is going on, when we connect the dots and see a greater truth revealed, it reminds us that we are connected to Infinite Intelligence. Wherever we are, IT is always right with us, doing ITs perfect work. IT truly wants nothing more than to experience ITself more greatly in physical form, in, through, and around us all.

As we realize this, we begin to see how connected we really are to others, and to all that is. We become larger, playing our part as co-creators in every aspect of our lives. We move into a greater experience of ourselves--our true, awesome, amazing selves--and experience more freedom and joy than ever before. This is what we yearn for. Thomas Troward in *The Edinburgh Lectures on Mental Science*, (1904), wrote,

> *The evolution which has brought us up to this standpoint has worked by a cosmic law of averages; it has been a process in which the individual himself has not taken a conscious part. But because he is what he is, and leads the van of the evolutionary procession, if man is to evolve further, it can now only be by his own conscious cooperation with the law which has brought him up to the standpoint where he is able to realize that such a law exists. His evolution in the future must be by conscious participation in the great work, and this can only be effected by his own individual intelligence and effort.*

As spiritual beings, we were created to express. It's a natural part of what we are: creative expressions of Life. We can't stop ourselves from expressing. It's what we do, no matter how hard we may try not to. We are expressing ourselves all the time, one way or another. Everything we do is an expression of who we are, and we love the freedom to express ourselves in the way we want. When we can't, we're frustrated and unhappy, because it's not our nature to hold back, to rein in the truth of our being. Our nature is to take in and put out in our own unique way, as part of the flow of life.

Our "work," then, is to express ourselves--through a relationship, our marriage, our family, our job or profession, a personal project we're working on, a situation or condition in our life, our life as a whole. Expression might come through a health challenge. Whether we're retired or not, we still have our work because we have a life. If we are here, on this plane of action, we will always be expressing in some way, if only to do those things that keep us going. If we're not participating in the world or expressing in some way, then it's over. Being in the world requires our participation. It is the natural flow of life.

Ultimately, we are here to get to know ourselves in a greater way and to see what we can do with what we have. Instead of wasting our energy, it is time for us to maximize it and make it work for us. As we invest more into whatever it is we're doing, we reap the rich rewards that are there for us.

My mother was good at this. She gave her all to everything she did, and her traditional Slovenian holiday sweet bread, that our family calls "petesa" (also known as potica), was out of this world!

Chop Wood, Carry Water

Petesa is an art form that's perfected each time it's made. My Yugoslavian grandmother taught her daughters and daughters-in-law to make it, and they all gave petesa their own distinct flair--perhaps adding a different ingredient, or a higher-quality ingredient, or changing a timing.

The energy bar of its day, petesa consists of walnuts or pecans and lots of butter and honey in a yeast dough that needs to rise at different stages. You get the picture: It's very rich and takes a long time to make. You really have to love to make petesa, because it requires much loving energy and focus.

Making petesa is a tradition in our family, and we still have it for special occasions, especially Christmas and Easter. My daughter Liz and my son Joseph make it, and even though he's only 11, Joseph often talks about the fine art of petesa-making.

The most interesting thing about this is that my mother didn't even like petesa! She spent hours making it just to please us, tasting it only enough to make sure it turned out well. With five children, it's not as though she didn't have other things to do. But she loved creating good foods, and her whole life was dedicated to loving, serving, and supporting her family. It made her happy. Memories of her love and dedication came back to me in her final days, helping me to respond with love when she wasn't feeling well or got a little cranky.

When I told my husband John that my mother didn't like petesa, he said, "That's really what it's about: Chop wood, carry water, serve others with good intention." That's what I want to remember about my mother; not the difficult parts when she was sick, but all the years and great gifts she gave us as we grew up. She will continue to be with us as we carry on the tradition and enjoy petesa, this delicious food for the soul.

Behind the Scenes

Like his grandmother, my son Nick gives his all to everything he does, which included a time in his life where he was a server at an exclusive restaurant on top of a mountain in Vail, Colorado. This was seasonal work, which allowed him to spend the rest of the year traveling and working elsewhere. From the start, he loved the area and work so much, he spent four years there.

Not everyone can afford to dine at such a high class restaurant, much less stay at the resort its part of. Those who can afford it expect royal treatment. Consequently, the work was intense and demanding, and in order to succeed, Nick gave each new day his all, creating a uniquely enjoyable experience for the people he waited on. He was "theirs" for as long as they were dining.

The end of Nick's fourth season at the restaurant was a transformational time for him: he got the itch for a new adventure and contemplated doing something different. We talked about it, and did treatment work--positive prayer. He soon realized that he wasn't quite ready for a change, and that sometimes it's better to wait until we really know what we want; otherwise, we get a mixed result. In the end, Nick decided to return to Vail for one last season. When he arrived, he received a warm welcome from the people he knew, and easily found a place to live. He felt good about returning to one of his "homes". Everything flowed. It was perfect.

This was no surprise. The treatment work we did together before Nick's very first season at Vail was still working on his behalf, because it was spoken from a loving place and with the best consciousness he could muster. This time with little effort, he continued to give the people he served great love and care.

Vail, and all that went with Nick's life there--working with fine foods at an exclusive restaurant, creating a unique dining experience for the guests he served, and snowboarding down the mountain during long breaks and at the end of the day, as well as on his off hours--was a demonstration of how what is originally created in mind expands with time. Whether he left for good at the end of the season or returned, Vail will always have a special place in Nick's heart. The time he invested there built his confidence and opened his mind to a vision of what's possible. This is a precious gift he has given himself that will live on wherever he goes. Kahlil Gibran wrote,

> *Work is love made visible. And if you cannot work with love but only with distaste, it is better that you should leave your work and sit at the gate of the temple and take alms of those who work with joy,*

Giving to Others

Freely sharing our talents and abilities is another way to express who we are. It feels good to give away what is important to us. When we give of ourselves by doing what we love, we are fed. We are inspired. We want to do more. We are proud of doing a good job. It makes a difference in us to be able to give in this way. Others benefit too, even if we never know it, and even if they won't, or can't, appreciate what we do for them. It may take years for them to "get it." That's okay. We give because it makes us feel good and it's ours to do. The Universe takes care of the rest, and we keep doing what's right for us to do, and stay focused on our work.

Like any other work, relationships require much of us. At one point, my husband John and I agreed that our son Joseph may be the most important work we're doing. When we thought about it that way, it was easier for us to give him our undivided attention.

Joseph has always been a strong spirit and a powerful creator. He demonstrates what he wants, and his list of wants is always a mile long. Like everyone else, he's seeking his good. You could say that getting what he wants is his work, his practice. You could also say that Joseph's continual wanting is an unfortunate effect of materialism.

As parents, we often think that we're working on our children. What a surprise when we discover that they are working on us! For though materialism may strike us as unhealthy, it's tough to regulate what's necessary and what's excess, and the more money people have, the more difficult that becomes. Also, there is a healthy way to look at materialism that is often missed, a wisdom that's needed. For example, we can appreciate modern appliances and technology. We can appreciate our comforts. Nothing wrong with that! We were given the ideas by the Creator ITself. Even our desires are natural, and given to us.

The problem lies in the unhealthy pursuit of more and more. It arises when having the latest and the greatest has become the reason to live, acquisition and possession the road to happiness. Of course, material things can't bring us happiness for long, and we soon move on to the next thing.

John and I can hardly be considered pushovers, and one of Joseph's closer friends believes we are stricter because we are ministers. Pondering this, I felt frustrated, and asked myself what Joseph's insatiable needs are about. I wondered what experience he thinks he's going to get from "stuff," what experience he's seeking. The answers to these important questions were right in front of me.

Most 11 year olds, especially those who live in the Disney capital of the world, as Joseph does, want to feel charged, alive. True to form, Joseph is a thrill seeker, and there isn't a roller coaster he won't try. He wants those things that give him instant gratification. Getting things makes him feel loved and important, a part of the flow. Seeing this, I also saw that I was tired of saying "no" or "we can't" even if we could. Constantly saying no to my son didn't feel good to me, especially since I teach abundance. I surely don't want to impose the limitations I grew up with on a budding creator.

This was hard work for me, and I decided to approach the situation from a different angle. I started by saying to Joseph, "There's no room in your bedroom to put things. Maybe if you get rid of some things, we can think about getting what you want." We started joking about how he must know something I don't: Even though his room appears to be normal size, the walls must expand when he's in there. He says he wants a tiger. I said, "Wow, you've got a jungle in there, too!" He laughed. It felt so good to both of us to break out of that old, stuck pattern. Even young creators have to know they have options and that they are living from possibility.

It felt good to support Joseph in this way, even though it was work. It required me to be present, focused, open, and receptive to a new way, and to come from love to do that. We were creating a new pattern of thinking and communicating, for Joseph doesn't know yet that he can feel charged and alive without all the things he thinks he needs. As he matures, he will find new ways to meet his great need to express and feel alive.

There's no doubt that living by design and not default is work, and that three strong spirits--Joseph, John, and I--living and expressing together is challenging. Our family dynamics can be intense, and they are always interesting. That may be why being together has dramatically changed us all for the better. We are mirrors for each other. We let each other know when we're "off" and we celebrate together when we're "on." We laugh at our mistakes and love each other no matter what. We have all learned and shared so much. We're more polished and more our true selves because of the work we've done together. We're both teacher and student to one another.

I can honestly say I would not be who I am today without living with Joseph and John.

Importance of Alignment

Since writing about Joseph's many wants and requests, I have heard Ester Hicks, who channels the Abraham teachings, talk about how important it is for parents to be aligned with their true, divine nature when they grant a child's request. For whatever reason, if the parents don't feel good about something a child wants, they need to honor their own feelings. Saying they aren't in agreement with the particular request at this time, because it doesn't feel right to them, teaches the child that it's important to honor our feelings. But if parents are out of alignment when they fulfill a request, they dishonor themselves and teach the child that we need to sacrifice for our loved ones. That isn't the message we want to teach.

It's also important for our children to be in alignment with their divine nature when they make a request. When they are, they will express how much fun it would be to have what they are requesting, what it would mean to them, and what it might mean to others. If they are out of alignment, they will focus instead on how much they need their request, and on convincing, persuading, begging their parents to grant it. When children receive while being out of alignment, they learn to go about getting what they want in the wrong way, and later in life wonder why they can't get what they want.

It may appear that we are our children's only source. In reality, Spirit is. Parents may be one of the main channels through which children receive their good, but they are not the only channel. In an infinite Universe, there are an infinite number of ways for everyone, including children, to receive their good. Spirit can be very resourceful.

Love Your Way Out

When I moved to Atlanta in the mid 80's, I was looking for a full time job and was placed by an agency into a big name company's collection department. Lucky for me, I didn't have to call the customers; I just processed the payments. I have always enjoyed working with numbers. I felt as though I were back at one of my earlier jobs at a bank. The work was okay even though it wasn't what I wanted to do. The question was, what did I want to do? I secretly wondered if I would ever find work that I could say I loved.

It was only a year after my divorce, and I was still finding my way. I felt fragile, and it didn't take much to upset me. What I needed most of all was a way to support myself and see my kids.

Atlanta is a beautiful city. The weather is much milder than up north, and I enjoyed the friendliness of the people. But smoking was still allowed in offices, and I was surrounded by people who smoked, which was very difficult for me. I complained. I couldn't breathe.

Another issue was that some of the women I worked with were exceptionally frustrated and moody, and some were lifers; years ago, they had landed what they considered to be a good job, the chance of a life-time--even if it sucked the life right out of them. They paid a high price for that decision, and so did everyone around them. Needless to say, I was motivated to get out as soon as something better came along.

Every week, I combed through the want ads and sent out dozens of resumes. Nothing happened. I kept on. I was determined. There had to be something better.

At that time, I was going to a technical school part-time, taking a computer language of all things. I had heard there was good money in the data processing field and I needed man-sized pay: I had child support and frequent plane fares. I wouldn't finish school for several more months, and that put me in an awkward situation because I wasn't quite ready for my new line of work.

I needed help, and found it in an early Sunday morning radio program that featured Dr. Kennedy Shultz, who would later be my teacher. My weekends were filled with studies but I still got up early to listen to this brilliant man's practical words of wisdom. I took copious notes. I memorized what he had to say. This was good stuff, and I was determined to learn everything I could possibly learn from him. I was hungry for spiritual sustenance. My life was a mess. In fact, what it really needed was a complete makeover. I was starting from scratch.

One morning I heard Dr. Schultz say, "Whatever you are stuck in, you are going to have to love your way out of. That is the only way. When you do that, Life will support you and find a way to promote you out of wherever it is you are into something better." Ah-ha! Now I had some direction. I could do this!

I knew I had to go back to that office Monday morning and give everything I did and everyone before me my best love and attention. I had to give up the desperate search for a job, stop whining and complaining, and love right where I was. Soon after I started doing that, the company brought in air filter machines and my department hired a temp named Carol, who was to become a key player in my life and a life-long friend. As soon as we met, we began spending time together, studying and having fun. It was great to have a buddy. As I learned things from the Sunday radio program, I shared them with Carol, and her life started coming together too.

In a very short amount of time, an unexpected sequence of events moved me into a more perfect job situation, which included the work I was preparing for in my studies. My new employer took me early. Thank you God!

If I hadn't made the changes I needed to make when I did, I might still be in that office today, exhausted and defeated. Or, I might have quit and gotten another job, or a series of jobs, just like the one I didn't want. I would have kept attracting the same thing to me. I may never have met John or gone on to my real work and met all of the beautiful people I know, because Life doesn't give us the green lights, the go-ahead, until we love our work however we are expressing it right where we are, and making the most out of it that we can.

Love your work. You may feel like quitting or running away; staying may be the last thing you want to do. But to avoid attracting the same situation in a different setting with a new cast of characters, it is best to turn your attitude around and leave the situation on the best possible terms. Then you can be finished forever with what you don't want and move on to your greater good.

We can trust the perfection of Life. That perfection is present everywhere, and in whatever we happen to be involved in. The sooner we understand this, the sooner we're able to appreciate heaven on earth. The longer it takes for us to get it, the longer we experience hell. Heaven and hell are states of mind that we create, and they are a choice. I know that is blasphemous to some. For me, it's empowering. If we can create our heaven and hell right here, we can change any situation we're in by changing our thinking about it. We don't have to wait until we die from this life before we can experience all the gifts of Spirit that are waiting for us to enjoy here. We don't need the concept of hell again, because it's no longer a part of how we see life. It simply ceases to exist.

The Creative Process

Whether we know it or not, the creative process is always at work. For example, some years ago, our daughter Liz and son Nick gave John and me a beautiful hand-carved giraffe.

I recently stopped for a moment to admire the giraffe in its place of honor on the mantle, as I have often done through the years. In that instant, it dawned on me that the first large animal I saw at Lake Manyara National Park in Tanzania early this year was a giraffe. Putting two and two together, I realized that the Creative Process went to work the day we placed the giraffe on the mantle, because every time I stopped to admire the giraffe, I thought of Africa and how much I wanted to go there some day. The Universe rewarded my unintentional creativity with the "real deal." That's how it works.

Creation can be fun. We are born creators. The work is in getting clear about what we need or want. Once we know that, we let it go and move on with our life. We follow whatever leads we get and let the Creative

Process work on our behalf. We have at our disposal our very own, exceptionally efficient and effective personal assistant. How great is that?

Whatever we love about our lives, we can enhance or create again if ever needed. Whatever we don't like about it, we can change and create anew. We can always start again. Every day is a new day. We can change our minds. We can do it over. We can tell a new story. We can re-script our old way of seeing to a more loving perspective. We can go up to the buffet table of life and choose again. That's the beauty of it all. We are never stuck with anything or anyone. All we have to do is stop and create again. There's always a better idea waiting for us. As much as we can conceive of enjoying, we can have. With every choice comes greater clarity. With greater clarity we get to know ourselves better and that's where it starts getting fun.

For as long as we are alive, we're always expressing in the world. It doesn't matter if you are very young or very old. It doesn't matter whether you are rich or poor. It doesn't matter if you are sick or well. There is work before you for you to do. You decide how your life will be. It takes a lot of energy to live well, and even more to let things fall where they may, to allow the wind to carry you here and there.

Keep on Creating

It takes energy to create. It's mental work, and it requires commitment, love, and focus. It's an effort, and it's definitely worthwhile. The only other option is letting our lives fall apart, because left on their own, they will.

For example, my mother was caught in what I am going to call a "condition warp", with her illness. She was holding her own, trying to stay positive. She kept her own house, said her prayers, and went to church. Every day, she put on makeup and got dressed. She did everything she could to make the best of the situation; *and* she was in react mode.

It was hard for my mother to avoid focusing on the conditions and circumstances of her failing body, and she talked about everything that was happening to her. It's hard not to react to outer physical conditions. It's a very difficult situation to be in, and it took tremendous effort and energy for my mother to do what she was doing. Yet it was not enough to turn things around.

Ideally, when we're in such challenging circumstances, we stop and insist on seeing the perfection that exists, love where we are, and have the clarity of mind to set a new intention. My mother couldn't do that. Until the very end, she was in denial about what was happening; at least, she never said anything to indicate otherwise. When asked what she wanted, she said, "Of course, I want to live." It may very well have been her time; her work here seemed to be finished but she denied the possibility that her life could be over. If she had been able to accept her end, she might have been able to prepare herself and family members for an easier transition.

In the final weeks she was pretty much confined to bed because of an infection in her leg. One night, returning from the bathroom she had a fall. As my brother carried her back to bed, she told him, "I am ready to go." In less than a week, she was gone.

My mother's story is not uncommon. When we focus more on conditions than on what we want, things deteriorate. Challenging as it may be, we always have the option of loving what *is*, as Byron Katie, author of "Loving What Is", writes. We can always choose to embrace whatever situation we are in and do the necessary love and forgiveness work, especially with ourselves: clean up any messes we helped create; take care of ourselves, and follow Spirit's lead.

As we make our way through whatever the challenge is--health, finances, a relationship, a job, or a spiritual crisis--we are led out of it and find ourselves in something entirely new. We can overcome anything. If we keep our eye on what's possible, we are amazed to see what turns up. We feel lighter, freer, and younger than ever before, at least in spirit. We are ready to live fully.

Staying filled up with good, life-giving ideas, being as conscious as we possibly can, having the courage to be honest about what we want or do not want, consciously creating, is what this game of life is about. The Bible says "Where there is no vision, the people perish." In other words, when we don't have a vision, things fall apart. And it's easier to stay on top of things all along than to try to tackle them when adverse conditions appear.

We are expressing all the way up to our end in this world. Unless we put more energy, thought, and feeling into what we're creating than in what we don't want, the scale tips away from our good. It takes work to stay alive. It takes courage, trust, and "Big Love" to believe that you can do it. But If I can do it, so can you.

Being Present is Powerful

In his book, *Make Me An Instrument Of Your Peace*, author Kent Nerburn related a beautiful, touching story that takes place in the early '80's, when he was a cab driver.

Nerburn wrote that in the wee hours one morning he picked up an old woman in response to her call. She asked him to drive around town so that she could have one last look, and they had a nice visit along the way. When they reach their destination--a hospice--she asked how much she owed and he said, "Nothing." She insisted on paying, he insisted that this one was on him, and she thanked him for giving her a moment of joy.

Nerburn squeezed the old woman's hand and left. Driving around aimlessly, he was happy that he was able to give to her in the way he did, and that he was sensitive enough to not miss what was going on. "I don't think I have done anything more important in my life than to have been able to serve that woman today," he thought.

Little things are important. It doesn't matter what we do, as long as we do it with great love and give it our best attention. Our presence is so important. It takes effort to stay present and give of ourselves in that way.

Everything we do, every part we play, is "us" carrying out the creative process of the Universe on the individual level. No job is insignificant. Each one has its own place. Everything we do is Spirit operating as us, through us, as much as we will allow.

The more we're conscious of this, the more we can work together. And the more we do that, the more exciting and wonderful it gets. Our lives have greater meaning, and our experiences are richer and fuller.

Being one with the Universe, we have access to everyone and everything. The One Universal Mind thinks through us as much as we will allow it to. We have access to unlimited creative power and intelligence. Think about that! Life, Spirit, God creates through us and experiences ITself in yet another new way. What we have created together so far is nothing compared to what is possible. We haven't seen anything yet.

Everything we are is expressed by our being. Many go through their whole lives not knowing who they are, afraid to be themselves, waiting for something outside of them to change before they reveal themselves. But we don't have to wait for the conditions around us to change; we don't have to wait for permission to be true to who we are.

Only you can give yourself permission to be who you really are. It doesn't matter what someone else thinks. It doesn't matter if you lose your job or relationship. When the longing to be true to yourself is so strong that you'll do whatever it takes to have that happen, in Love and under the Law of the Universe, you will be free to be yourself.

Being free to be yourself means being free..to be true to yourself, to your needs, to your requirements, to your nature. Being free to how it is that you express in the world through your work, your play, how you communicate, what you do, what you stand for. You will know that your life's path, your spiritual path, is unfolding perfectly when you continually feel greater freedom and joy in being yourself. The more you do this, the happier you will be.

Born a Success

Some people spend their lives trying to prove themselves through long hours and hard work. What would it be like to believe that you are already perfect? You are already a success. That's where to begin, because it's the truth about you. You were created perfect by an amazing Universe. Give up the idea that you could ever have been born with sin or that it could possibly be a mistake that you are here. Everything and everyone has a purpose, even if we don't know yet what that could be.

When we're our true selves, we're in alignment with Source and our success is guaranteed. There's no need for rules and regulations or do's and don'ts to keep us in line. We were created with an internal guidance system that tells us how we're doing. When we recognize a spiritual authority within us, we can depend on it to lead us the right way.

We are already a success. We were born a success. We can't afford to accept negative things that other people say, or that we tell ourselves, because it drains us of our life force. It depletes us emotionally, physically, mentally and spiritually. These are merely distractions, blocks to our greater experience. If we remember that we are already perfect and in right and perfect relationship with Spirit, we can easily put anything else behind us, just as Jesus did when he said, "Get behind me Satan"

(Matthew 16:23). Get behind me, ways of the world, distractions, ideas, thoughts, and beliefs that get me off track. You have no power over me. I AM.

My first two children were not baptized. Though I was brought up Catholic, I could never believe that a pure, perfect, innocent baby could possibly be born in sin. I couldn't believe that if they died without being baptized, they'd go to "limbo," the place between heaven and hell. It didn't make sense to me, and I wanted no part of it.

Later, I heard through the grapevine that in the privacy of their own home and in their own way, my parents baptized my children. When I first learned this I felt angry, but my anger didn't last for long. I knew that my parents had acted out of love. They wanted only to protect my children, and a blessing certainly couldn't hurt them.

By the time Joseph came along, 16 years later, I was able to look at baptism as a welcoming of him into our community and the world. I felt honored that my teacher, Dr. Kennedy Shultz, performed the ceremony, which included creating a time capsule. Joseph's family and friends filled it with words of wisdom and love for him.

A failure is not necessarily a person who is bankrupt. A failure is anyone who, either through his own ignorance, or through his acceptance of situations apparently beyond his control, has resigned himself to some form of expression which is frustrating rather than creative. This causes an emotional conflict in his subconscious mind, producing lack of ease, a sense of guilt, and a feeling of insecurity.

Dr. Raymond Charles Barker
Treat Yourself to Life

You are a success if you are doing a creative job in life and can live without emotional strain in the economic and social pattern in which you find yourself.
The mighty are often brought low, but when they know what to do, they become again the mighty. They use rightly the only thing they have, thought and feeling. They realize that there is no judgment, no condemnation, no hell and no hell fire.
They recognize that the Infinite Spirit, the Divine Presence, and the inner thought are always saying "Be Positive."

Dr. Raymond Charles Barker
Power of Decision

103

Sacred Service

Being involved in a great idea--a life-giving, electrifying idea--allows us to make a small difference; or even a significant contribution. This is what has kept my Aunt Betty going. About to turn 78, she just got voted in for the tenth year to be the head of the seniors group at her church. She has also been running a food pantry for years, and this week, she's going to a luncheon sponsored by an organization that will present her with a nice check for the pantry.

I have always appreciated Aunt Betty's spunkiness. She recently told me that she continues to do service because she sees the great need--and because no one else will step up. Many older people don't get involved because they aren't feeling well. For her, serving or giving or being involved helps de-emphasize her aches and pains, which seems to lessen them and keeps her active.

Sometimes we simply can't leave home because of physical problems, transportation, or some other reason.

Sometimes we don't know what we could do as a volunteer, or where to start.

Sometimes, young or old, we feel as if we can't put one more thing on our plate. Our life is busy enough, and it's hard to imagine adding one more thing. Someone mentions volunteer work and we cringe.

Sometimes we can give more than we can at other times, especially if we're in a lull or have an opening that we didn't have before.

For whatever reason, not everyone can contribute in the way my aunt can. But it doesn't matter, because sacred service doesn't have to be a big thing. It can be a very small thing done with great love, as Mother Teresa used to say.

In any case, serving doesn't work if we do it out of obligation or because we feel pressured. It doesn't work if we serve because we think it may look good on our resume', or because our friends are doing it and we wouldn't measure up if we didn't. Serving because we can't say no or because religious teachings say that service is important and will help us prosper or feel better are also not good enough reasons.

To be meaningful, service has to be done for the right reasons, and it really needs to work for us. The degree to which we can serve depends on what's going on in our lives.

It's well known that Jesus went to the desert when he was exhausted. It was a place of rest and replenishment, and as author and speaker, Wayne Muller, puts it, that would not be a good time to go calling upon him for a miracle. The same is true for us. We have to be in the right place with ourselves in order for the giving to really benefit the one we are serving. Otherwise, we aren't going to want to do it. We have to see the value we are giving, and it needs to feed us in some way.

We aren't here to suffer, to give up, to make sacrifices. That's fruitless work. Unless our service flows for us, it doesn't benefit anyone--least of all, ourselves. We serve the world by being the best we can, by working on ourselves, by creating a nice life for ourselves, by being peaceful, and by giving love wherever we can. The gift is in the giver and we all have something to give even if it is to ourselves. Seeing ourselves as a contributor makes us a part of a bigger picture than just our own lives.

It All Works Together

At 21, I was a newlywed. My husband and I lived in a small town called Burlington, outside of Milwaukee, where he worked. There were few jobs besides working in a factory or restaurant. Definitely there was nothing in my field. Bored to tears, I wondered what I had gotten myself into and what I could do about it

Looking for a more meaningful way to express myself, I volunteered at a social service center in town. They were happy to have me. I supported a woman who was responsible for cases throughout the county. We became fast friends. The days she came to town, she picked me up in the morning and we were off, running around the countryside, making whatever work visits she needed to, and enjoying each other's company. Thirty-four years have passed and we are still connected. I am forever grateful to my friend and former co-worker for saving my spirit those many years ago and putting my energies to a good cause.

We never know who may become a friend for a long time. We never know how we will feel when we give what we can. We never know where service will lead us. Though it's not the reason to do service, when we give it our best, put our whole self into it, the Universe takes care of the rest.

At times, there's something right before us that we can do. But we don't feel up to it, and someone else does it. If we realize later that missed a chance to do something important, it doesn't matter. There will be another chance.

I like what author Piero Ferrucci wrote in *The Power of Kindness*: "Tomorrow another opportunity will arise; a friend will be feeling lonely, there'll be dinner to cook, a scared child to comfort. I will be ready."

Serving others brings out the best in us all. It's the only way to live.

Moving On

You're not a bad person for leaving a job, project, or partnership and moving on. Life is forever calling us into greater expression and experience, helping us to know ourselves in a greater way. As infinite beings, that will always be so for us. We will always want to know more about who we are. We will always want to be becoming more than we know ourselves to be. It is the nature of Life.

We're never happy when we hold ourselves back. Our decisions are nothing personal to anyone else. We don't owe anyone our life. We don't have to commit ourselves to anything or anyone forever. Our creative expression depends on us following the inner voice of wisdom within us, and the path that is perfect for us to take. We owe it to ourselves to be true to who we are. By expressing our very best and following Spirit's lead, we give the world around us a great gift: permission to do the same.

Wouldn't the world be a much healthier, better place if people were happy with themselves, doing what they loved, and honoring what wanted to come through them?

Today, as I write this book, our country is experiencing great financial challenges. Many have been laid off and are without work. Many companies have folded. People have been re-thinking what is really needed to exist, and downsizing. They have had to shift their ideas about how to earn a living. New startup businesses have begun. While many are worried about what will happen to them and their families, this shakeup invites us all to take another look at how we're creatively approaching the challenges that come our way.

Beautiful new opportunities are unfolding, opening up new spaces within us, and in our lives, for greater living. One woman I know is renting rooms in her home, starting a new business with online greeting cards, and she and her family have created a tasty new recipe to market publicly. Everything that happens is good. There's a divine purpose to it all. All we need to do is see how perfect it is. All we need to do is see ourselves for who we really are. Instead of just reacting, we can embrace all the changes, knowing they help us to know ourselves in ways we could not have guessed. What could be greater than that? It's time to be the beautiful, creative expressions we came here to be. It is time to see what we can create together.

We are the guests of an invisible Host whose presence we feel and whose form we shall see when our eyes are opened to the fact that it clothes itself in innumerable forms. It is our business to unite, not to divide; to include, not to exclude; to accept, and not to renounce.

Ernest Holmes
Science of Mind

I Can Do This Thing Called Work -- and So Can YOU!

Mind Treatment – Perfect Expression

Step 1:

I live in a Universe that expresses perfectly in each and every one of IT's creations.

Step 2:

I am a perfect creative expression of the One.

Step 3:

I am always in my right and perfect place, doing work I love that brings out the very best of me.

Step 4:

Nothing gets in the way as I perfectly express my gifts and talents in the world.

Step 5:

I give my best energy, love, and attention to all that I do and the Universe promotes me into something greater when I am ready.

Step 6:

I give thanks for knowing that I am a wonderful contributor to my world.

Step 7:

And so it is!

7
I Can Do This Thing Called Wealth

Years ago I began my morning by writing about my ideal day. This is what I wrote:

I wake up refreshed after a good night of sleep. The air is cooling. Autumn is in the air. Change is there too. It's the perfect day for a grand shift to take place in the paradigm we humans have been living under. Today is the perfect day for Spirit to break loose in us all and be set free. The old paradigm falls away overnight. Old patterns of thought lose their hold on us forever. Darkness is lit by the Eternal Light.

A new paradigm is born and becoming stronger and more powerful by the minute. We now live as spirit, in Spirit. New doors are opened. Opportunities abound for everyone. Everyone's basic needs are taken care of. Energies are spent in new ways on new ideas.

Today, my family and I live this Reality. I require that my needs be met on an instant and ongoing basis. Today, I am open and receptive to large sums of money that allow me to be all that I can. I am free in the Now moment. My energy is used on creation and offering support to others regarding better ways of living. My purpose is clear. My role is perfectly played. Right opportunities and right money are mine today. There's an opening where a door was closed before. The Infinite Wisdom of God knows how to support ITself as me, and as my family. We listen. We know exactly what to do. I listen. I know exactly what I need to know and what to do. I insist on staying in the Truth. I am unshakeable, well-grounded, and fearless. I am love, power, strength and wisdom, right here and now.

I believe there is a receptiveness within us large enough to allow great wealth. I have faith the size of a mustard seed. I am strong. I am a center of divine activity. I am in right relationship with God. I am in right relationship with my higher self, with my husband, with my work.

Thank you God for being with us today and showing us what you can do. I believe you are there and you know exactly how to open more channels for us today. Thank you God for taking care of us so magnificently in order that we may truly serve you from that rich place within us. And so it is!

Ideal days are a form of prayer, a mind treatment. They put you in a co-creative partnership with the Universe. They are a series of positive statements of what you would like to see. If you do this on a regular basis, you will experience significant shifts in the way you think and what you see and experience. These are life changing, and not necessarily in a way that we expect.

When I wrote about my ideal day, my intention was to shift my consciousness, open up my thinking, break out of my trapped, limited worldview, my little world. It was designed as a series of steps to move myself through confused or distorted thinking. If my thinking was clear, positive, and powerful, I would appreciate the results I was seeing, at least in that particular area of my life.

But I was not so happy with our financial picture. In fact, I was quite distressed over the experience we had been having, not knowing where our money was coming from at any given time or how much we could count on. I knew I needed to take a stronger approach to the mental work I had previously done. I was ready for serious results, and a more consistent, steady flow of income. What came out of me with that mental work that day felt very powerful and clear.

I did say in my Ideal Day that I was ready to demonstrate, and to take my family right along with me on a new adventure.

All hell broke loose after that. Work came to a screeching halt. John's consulting work stopped. My income diminished. Life as we knew it stopped. We had depended on credit cards a little too much. It was nothing frivolous, just survival. Two freelancers in the family without a fully developed prosperity consciousness created quite a challenge.

Well, for the first time in our lives, we were maxed out and couldn't pay. It was time to cut up the charge cards. There were no longer cards to fall back on. Now we had to demonstrate everything on an as-needed basis. We had forced the issue. We had to trust that we were supported from a higher place.

Being independents, our health care coverage had gone beyond what we could pay. No more health insurance. Literally, we could not afford to get sick. We had to stay healthy. It was up to us! There was deeper work to do. All those places where we were out of alignment with those beautiful ideas of truth stated in my Ideal Day showed us exactly what work we needed to do.

I am not sure why I was surprised by how things happened. Old ways and habits must fall apart before the new ones can take their place. I had seen the power of prayer in action before. It had never happened so quickly and powerfully as this did. I guess I was still questioning whether all that really came from me. There was a part of me that didn't believe that I had asked for all this and that it really was a part of a new, larger picture I had been wanting to see.

We should always expect to see something happen as the result of our prayers. People say they pray and at the same time don't believe their prayer will be answered. Because they believe this way, they don't see any connection between what they really want and what is playing out all around them. Prayers always demonstrate if they are done the right way, and from the right place. Always expect to see something happen, even if it doesn't look like what you asked for. There is always something greater trying to happen. If it isn't quite what you had in mind, get clearer about what it is you do want, and claim that.

Now, I don't recommend demonstrating as drastically and quickly as we did, unless you are really ready to go with a faster-moving current. It is possible to demonstrate with greater grace and ease, but what we experienced was the immediate power of positive prayer or treatment. We definitely got what we asked for and it meant that we had some cleaning up to do, and some aftermath to contend with. We needed to make some changes in the way we were doing things and in the way we were living. What we didn't know at the time was that we were in the midst of an intense, amazing and incredible transformation. From this time forward, we would be operating on a new level that required us to trust and know Spirit, as our Source, like never before.

Some of us have a high tolerance for living with things as they are; and then, when we have had it up to our eyeballs, we blow. Sometimes, it takes getting stuck in a corner or having things fall apart before we make the necessary changes. There are times when immediate and intense shifts are very effective. Certain situations call for it. Some of us also have to learn more about not waiting so long and putting off what we need to do the first time we get the gentle nudge. There is always a reminder. There is that within us that always knows what is best and is trying to get our attention. As you go along, this becomes easier. As you fine-tune your consciousness, you will clear away the major interference.

Lots of love and forgiveness are necessary for all of our experiences and discoveries along life's journey.

One Infinite Source

Typically we look to our job, family, husband, or partner, bonuses or income tax returns, or retirement, social security, or inheritance as the source of our financial income. Many times, those ways do take care of us very well; it is all working and the money continues to flow.

But when our sources of income dry up, or become less than we have grown accustomed to for the life style we are living, we have to really take a look at who is our source and get straight about that.

We will always get into trouble if we believe that any outside channels are our source. They can never be. They are merely channels for our good, wonderful as they are. There can only ever be one source of our good and that is the Universe or God. When we know that, we can more easily see that while channels of income will come and go, there is a Source that is infinite and endless and always there for us. We need only ever to go directly to our real Source.

When we know that, or continue to remind ourselves that God is our Source, we will also know that we can never be forgotten or left out in any way. When we have this idea that God is our Source firmly established in our minds, it won't matter what is happening to us on the outside, because we know that we are well-provided for, loved, and supported.

We will also see that though we are channels for good, we are not the ultimate source for anyone—not for our children or anyone else who believes that we are. Although we have often assumed that role because we believed we were their source. Knowing our place and our part empowers everyone. Helping our children see that God is their source, and their supply does not really come from us is a real gift we can give them. They, too, will have to move into working with their true Source and learn to take responsibility for themselves.

Learning that God is my Source was a huge realization for me. It continues to make a powerful difference in my life. I know it will for you as well.

Abundance is Life's Way

One Sunday morning, Timmy, a young boy in our youth program, shared his experience of seeing a large sea turtle laying eggs. He was excited about this, as you might imagine. Mother turtle was three feet long and laid about a hundred eggs. She does this three or more times a summer, and the rangers cover up the nest with a wire fence to keep the raccoons out. It takes about sixty days for the baby turtles to hatch and make their way to the ocean. Only one out of a thousand makes it to maturity.

Timmy told us that the mother is really unconcerned if a raccoon eats some of her eggs. Concerned or not, these turtles are generally fairly big and move slowly on land; they don't appear to have much of a defense for themselves or their eggs.

When you think of it, why would a mother turtle care if a raccoon wants to get in on the act when all of nature is so abundant? There is plenty for everyone. So what if someone gets their dinner early? Everyone has to eat and there is plenty for all, including us. What a lesson for us all.

Abundance is Our Nature

Abundance is everywhere. Look around. Nature's abundance is obvious in springtime. There is evidence everywhere. We are one with nature, so that is our truth, too. What is true on one level of existence has to be true on all levels. Nature's way is our way.

Why do we have such a hard time understanding that? It may have something to do with the way we were brought up. Several centuries of industrialization and materialization, and looking at the universe as a machine or a thing, impersonal, different, and separate from ourselves, has played havoc with our consciousness. It is time for that to be healed. Everything is alive. We can never be separate. We are all living the One Life. We have to get that perception right before things can really change in our lives. We are not alone in the world, making it all happen. We are interconnected with all of life. All of life works together. All of life is conspiring on our behalf. IT wants us to succeed. IT is working with us at every given moment.

Plato said, "To understand is to perceive patterns." There are definite laws, or ways that life works, that apply to us all. It would be great for us to get to know them, so that we don't continue to butt our heads against a wall trying to figure things out. There's a definite pattern here, if we will only look and see.

Ebb and Flow

The ache we feel, the void we feel, the loss or the pain we feel when the tide goes out and it looks like we are without is often mistaken as bad. We say, "Oh, look here I am again. My checkbook is empty, I am back where I started, I always end up here, or Why does this have to happen to me?" All this is really a misinterpretation of what is really going on. We live in an Intelligent Universe. We must approach it intelligently.

If we could see that an ebb is a part of a cycle, just as much as flow, we would see that it is normal. If we saw that it is very much like breathing, we wouldn't get so worried. We would continue to feel alive. We can't keep taking in air without letting out air. We can't keep taking in our good, our money, our energy, our love without expressing and circulating it. We would implode or burst. Living without giving is not part of the Divine Health Care Plan or the Universal Bank.

If we could see how normal this cycle is, we wouldn't freak out and go into a panic and put ourselves in opposition to the flow the minute it happened. Instead, we would allow ourselves to be in it.

Breathing is an easy release: taking in, releasing continually. We don't even know we are breathing unless we hold our breath. When we hold our breath, symbolically, by our negative reaction, we stop the flow of circulation of good and money in our lives. When we freak out or get stuck in our fear, things stop cold in their tracks and we experience shortage, lack and even the end of our flow. We jump to conclusions, think the worst, give our full attention to what is wrong, and spiral downward from one thought to another.

The magic that can end this downward spiral is to believe that we are an important part of the one Life we are all living together; to know that we are always perfectly taken care of and can trust that whatever is happening will turn out for the better, that new avenues of income and opportunity will open up to us. Staying positive, we discover that Life is Good and IT is always for us, conspiring on our behalf.

Our ache, our void, our pain is our sacred yearning for the divine, to be closer, to experience more of it.

Opportunities to Deepen

Our prosperity problems are always a call to go deeper into our spiritual truth, and we do that through spiritual practices. How spiritually fed are we? Do we feel loved and supported? Do we have love and energy for ourselves as well as others? Or are we running on empty? Maybe we have been running on next to nothing for years. Are we choking the life right out of us by denying ourselves the benefits of living a good life? Maybe we don't have a clue as to how to take care of ourselves. Maybe we never learned.

There was a point in my own life where I had said "no" to spending money on myself so many times that I found I couldn't say "yes." It didn't take long before I got the hang of that one again. Our nature is a desiring one. We must learn to honor that and work with it. It doesn't mean we have to acquire and possess everything we desire. It means we can appreciate the life that surrounds us, and find balance in the things we want around us.

What are you doing in the form of spiritual practices, every day, to keep in touch with your real self? Positive prayer, meditation, reading, setting your intentions, visualizing, visioning are all great practices. Start somewhere. It may be as simple as taking a walk in nature, going fishing, or playing golf. Whatever it is that brings you joy. If you want to see prosperous results in your life, you have to spend time every day being quiet, taking time out, doing something you love or that makes you feel uplifted.

Whatever you choose to do is good. You will begin to open up, feel freer, breathe easier, and feel yourself. You will begin to see possibility where you couldn't before. The more you see and feel, the more you will want to do, and the more you will put yourself in Life's flow.

The clearer you get about who you are and…what your purpose is, what value you bring to the world…the more you will be a magnet for possibility, opportunity, money, wealth, and health. Life will not be able to resist you.

Natural Born Creators

Life is all about recognizing that you were born a creator, designed and equipped to create; that you create your true heart's desire and more of what you want, instead of focusing your energies on what you don't want and creating more of that.

You may say, "Well, how can I create when I don't have any money." Take some steps in that direction. There are always some preliminary things that can be done. Spend time thinking about them. Envision what you want happening with you in the picture. What does living like this feel like? What could it do for you, your family, and others around you to have money? Money or whatever else we want follows a good idea not the other way around. We must create first, in mind. Be clear about what you want, get excited about it, and claim it. It's yours!

The "I Am" Presence As You

"Be still and know that I AM." In other words, Don't panic, worry, or bury yourself in fear. "Be Still" stops all the crazy, destructive thoughts and helps us to center on the power of the words, "I Am." All we have to do is recognize that God is, Life is, Spirit is. We are the I Am Presence as us, We are One. We are unique individuals, creative expressions of Spirit. When we know that, we will know that we are always taken care of and in God's flow.

Never About Money

The first time I heard that it's never about money, I got mad. It was difficult not to get mad. "What do you mean, it's not about money? I don't have enough. If I had the money, my problems would be solved. How can it not be about money?" To me, it was all about money.

Money is not the solution to our difficulties, even though we think it would make a huge difference having some. Getting huge sums of money is never the answer. It will take us more comfortably from point A to point B, but that may keep the very thing that needs to happen from happening: a change of consciousness, a greater belief in ourselves, knowing we can do what we really want to do. We can enjoy it all. We were meant to enjoy it all. Money can't do that for you. Only you can do that for yourself.

Limitation is Not Our Truth

We were never meant to live in limitation. We were never meant to have to watch every penny we spend. We were never meant to have to bargain hunt (as a way of life), or be afraid that we'll be cheated, or pay our bills late, or hold onto our money as long as we can because we don't know when we will have some again. Did I forget any?

There are so many things we tolerate and accept. We don't even think of changing them. We do all kinds of things for money at the expense of ourselves, our health, and our well-being. We put up with all kinds of things we should never tolerate for the wrong reasons. But in reality, we can have it all, enjoy doing what we love, and enjoy financial wealth. What a relief that is to know.

Positioning Ourselves

Nothing opens us up more to receiving our abundance than giving, even if all we have to give is praise or a simple thank you note.

Always ask, "What do I need to know or do today that will give me a greater sense of freedom, make me feel good, help me to feel prosperous?" Then, listen and do what you feel guided to do. Maybe lighting a candle helps you feel like you are capturing a divine moment. Maybe buying yourself some fresh-cut flowers makes you feel indulgent and rich. Treating yourself to a nice meal is a rich idea. Light a candle and turn your bill paying into a sacred experience. Take the time to enjoy the preparations along the way in whatever you do. See what ideas come to you from that.

Always have a secret stash of money you can spend on yourself, even if it is only $20. A good friend, Rev. Pat King,, shared that with me during our difficult financial crunch. This is money to spend on yourself for whatever you want, even when there are bills to pay. I know that sounds indulgent and even irresponsible. That makes it even more fun. We ourselves must be taken care of and there is only one person who can do that: ourselves. We must feel rich in order to keep the prosperity lines open.

If I were to wish for anything, I should not wish for wealth and power, but for the passionate sense of the potential, for the eye which, ever young and ardent, sees the possible. Pleasure disappoints, possibility never. And what wine is so sparkling, what so fragrant, what so intoxicating as possibility!

Soren Kierkegard - Harvest Time

Several years ago, I attended the opening ceremony and dedication of the Dr. Bobbie Bailey and Family Performance Center for Kennesaw

State University, just outside of Atlanta. This $9 million facility houses 624 seats, a gallery, and a rehearsal hall. All kinds of musical creations take place in this inspired setting.

The performance center is beautiful, well-designed, and acoustically perfect. The stage is huge, and high lofts in the back and front easily accommodate special pieces and parts. The center of the room is used for readings, and the exquisite design places the audience right smack in the middle of all the action.

At the center of the stage is a magnificent Steinway piano, dedicated to the Bailey family's mother, who played hymns for her children when they were young.

What a celebration! What a harvest! This was a clear demonstration of Dr. Bobbie Bailey's lifetime of dedication and commitment to excellence. It came about because several years earlier, the past principal of the university asked Dr. Bailey if she would help with the planning and funding of a performance center, which the dean of the school of music had dreamed of for 35 years. She said "Yes," and together, they made it happen.

Some demonstrations are immediate, some take a day, some take years, and some seem to take an eternity. Many will not be seen in our lifetimes. Demonstrations are our harvests, the results of those seeds we have planted and cultivated. It was Dr. Bailey's dream to invest the fruits of her labor—her money, time, and attention—into something worthwhile, something of great value, with longevity.

At the close of her speech, Dr. Bailey said with obvious excitement that the performance center was to be a Steinway School. This meant that 98% of the pianos must be Steinways, and that she had just donated 25 more pianos.

Only a lifetime of planting seeds every day could produce the demonstrations I witnessed that day in Atlanta. It took years and years of working with a higher purpose in mind to have the means to give such a gift, one that will benefit many people for years to come.

The Secret to Wealth

We live in a world that is about getting, and many people think they are owed something. "What's in it for me?" they ask. What they don't realize is that you don't *get* in life unless you *give* first. The question needs to be "What kind of contribution can I make to my world and all those around me?"

It's not that we shouldn't get. We should! But our first emphasis needs to be on what we bring to the table. "What's in it for me" will naturally follow when we come to life each day as a giver first.

After we give, or even intend to give, we get. The getting is in the giving, and you receive immediately by the act. You feel good about yourself. You open yourself up to greater circulation of good. You create a vacuum that will quickly be replaced with something of equivalent or greater value than what you originally gave. You must always give to get. You must sow the seed before you can reap the harvest. What you plant today, you will harvest at a later time. Guaranteed. That's the way Life works.

What did the philanthropist, Dr. Bailey, who created this magnificent performance center get from the harvest? The school dedicated a scholarship program in her name to provide monies for continued education for arts students. Even more than that, her dreams came true. She used her harvest to bring the arts into more people's lives, and thus share it with the world. The fulfillment of her heart's desire is the grand prize. It doesn't get much better than that. I am sure that when she was planting her seeds long ago, she had no idea that someday her harvest would truly be food for the soul.

Don't judge each day by the harvest you reap but by the seeds that you plant.

Robert Louis Stevenson

The Land of Good and Plenty

Douglas Jerroid, an English humorist, playwright and journalist, wrote "Earth is so kind, that you just tickle her with a hoe and she laughs with a harvest."

It's true. Earth is very fertile. She loves to create. That's how the Universe works and that is how we work. We just have to tickle the Creative Medium of the Universe—universal soil, so to speak—with a thought and it goes forth to produce it. All it takes is a tickle in the right direction, one that meets our fancy, and the Law of Life brings it about.

Compound Interest

There would be no advantage to be gained by sowing a field of wheat if the harvest did not return more than was sown.

Napoleon Hill
Think and Grow Rich

We can always count on the harvest being more than we have sown because that is how the Universe works. That is the Law of Growth. IT is always expanding. IT always gives us more than we have asked for, and takes us up a level to experience more than we have before. IT gives us an incentive to live more greatly, and then to expand on what we can give the next time. IT works with us and grows us. We are infinite beings. We will continue to grow and expand forever as long as we get out of our own way. As we grow and strengthen, so does our capacity. We are given more, and then there's more for us to give. We can do more, with grace and ease.

Our harvests grow as we do. At times, we think we are ready to immerse ourselves in the big picture up front. We get into trouble trying to rush the process. We lose sight of what is really important. In this country, it seems everything is about bigger and better: having more toys, making a quick dollar. We are more interested in huge yields from which we can make more money than in producing a good product. We forget that the product is only as good as the love and consciousness we put into everything we do. That is quite a different focus.

If the fruit or vegetable is filled with pesticides that are harmful to humans, or genetically engineered to produce a big crop that causes us physical problems, we have missed the point. We may very well have produced what appears to be a "greater harvest" or big yield. We may have produced something that can stay on the shelf for days, weeks, or months. But is it really a greater harvest if the nutritional value is compromised? Shouldn't the goal be to produce strong, healthy bodies, and food that supports us in being all we can be in the world? We lose sight of what is really important. We may get what appear to be great results but not the kind of results we could be get if we thought only about what the product does for the consumer and the environment.

The same is true in our own lives. We need to take the right next steps with an end in mind that truly benefits the greater good of all. We are never given more than we can handle. There is a process to our growth.

Sometimes we just have to love where we are and love what is. We can't rush growth as much as we think we can; and what is the big hurry, anyway? There is always plenty of Life to enjoy right where we are. When we live Life according to IT's design, we will grow spiritually, and the result of that is greater self-esteem, plenty of money, a quality product or service we can be proud of, making a difference in our world, personal satisfaction, and happiness.

When we work for the greater good of all, there is no more delicious delight than reaping the fruits of our labor. It makes everything we did to get there worthwhile.

Harvests Are Guaranteed

Everything we do in life contributes to our harvest. We really never have to worry about that. The harvest will be as good as the love, energy, and consciousness we put into each thing we do every day. Planting the seeds and nurturing them to full maturity is our work. The rest takes care of itself. Something good will come of it all.

During my visit to Atlanta to participate in the opening ceremony of the Dr. Bobbie Bailey & Family Performance Center, I was able to see and enjoy some harvests of my own. This included a growing relationship with my cousin there. Twenty-three years earlier, he had introduced me to this new kind of spirituality where I found my real home.

Even though we don't see each other often, we talk when we can. He has always been loving and supportive, and encouraged me every step of the way. No matter how much time passes before we get together again, we easily pick up right where we left off.

So many years later, I saw first hand what this teaching and way of life has done for my cousin, his health and well-being, his travels and his home. Once again we enjoyed our precious time together, talking about all we were learning and how we were putting it to work for us. It's great having such a wonderful relationship, especially with a member of your own family.

I also had the opportunity to see and spend time with my dear friend Carol, who was my date for the dedication dinner and ceremony.

Carol and I met years before in the accounting department of a major company in Atlanta. Even though it was a temporary position, we couldn't wait to get out of there, and we supported each other as we picked up the pieces of our lives and learned how to create a new life for ourselves. At that time, she was attending night school at Kennessaw State University.

We have maintained our long distance relationship all these years and have been there for each other in many ways. I appreciated her loving support and friendship.

The special night started with a private dinner for family, friends, and those involved intimately in the creation of this building and event. Much to our surprise, the past president of the school came over to our table to meet Carol after hearing that she was one of their graduates. Carol beamed. How far she had come and how much she had grown. She created a whole new life she herself which included a family of her own. I relished it all. I was sitting next to grace and beauty itself.

Harvests are all around us. They are the natural outcome of what we give. We just have to recognize them and take time to appreciate them. There are many ways in which we give our love and attention. We contribute to people, causes, and projects. Even giving in small ways makes a difference. Some of our harvests come years later as a big surprise. Sometimes we say something that we don't give another thought to and it changes someone's life completely. This is all part of our harvest. Everything we give comes back to us multiplied abundantly.

Making the Most of What We Have

I don't think we can all create at the level of giving millions. I do think we can create at our own level. Everyday we have opportunities to plant seeds, to take care of what is before us with great love. What we do with what we have is more important than how much we give. If we give from a place of obligation, pressure or resentment, our gift is not the same as if we give freely, easily and generously of all we have. How we give makes all the difference. My son, Nick, would give the shirt off of his back to anyone who asked. He doesn't have a lot of material goods. Yet, he is a very rich man.

We should live and labour in our times that what comes to us as seed may go to the next generation as blossom, and what came to us a blossom may go to them as fruit. This expresses the true spirit in the love of mankind.

Henry Ward Beecher, 1813-1887
American Clergyman, Editor, Abolitionist

It's important to remember that we are all at different places with our giving. The important thing is to begin giving where you are and stretch that as you continue giving. Your capacity will expand as you do that and you will find your capacity to receive more will as well. That is an added gift.

It's also important to remember that things are at different stages. Some gifts we get are the seeds of new ideas that will take a lifetime to bloom. Some projects will need to be passed on and taken over by others. Other gifts or creations we participate in are farther along in their maturation. If we can take the gifts we are given and do everything we can to bring them to the next level, we are doing well. This way, each generation benefits from what has been done before.

Small Thinking Sabotages

Nothing gets in the way of our harvests more than small thinking: Asking "What's in it for me?" "Why would I do that for the generations to come, who are they to me?" "Why would I want to do that?" Or saying, "I'm not seeing any benefits. This isn't working." Or even asking, "Where am I going to get the money?" or "When I win the lottery, I will do nice things for the world" are all examples of limited thinking.

Small thinking doesn't see the harvest; it tries to manipulate every little thing that happens.

We don't have to worry about where the money is coming from.

We don't have to know how to make money or how to bring it into our lives. We just have to do whatever we do with great love, take care of ourselves, practice staying positive, stay open, listen, follow our inner guidance, and allow ourselves to participate in the world by giving our best gifts.

Design or Default

What separates the people that live by design from those that live by default?

They keep on going. They keep on planting. They don't wait.

They trust that they are doing the right thing and always giving their best.

They follow their inner guidance.

They act for the right reasons. They genuinely want to see something good take place and support it.

They aren't doing it to have their name on a building—that's part of the gift back, but not the reason. Having one's name publicly displayed helps show others what is possible and inspires them to put their fruits to good use.

They want to know that their life had meaning and that they are leaving a legacy for the generations to come.

They have huge generous hearts.

They believe in themselves.

They believe they can make a difference.

They work with others to accomplish bigger projects.

They know the resources are there, even when they don't know exactly where.

Wealth is the Natural Outcome

Money is the natural outcome, or harvest, of clearing the fields, planting the seeds, watering and fertilizing the plants. That's the way it works every time.

We aren't here on this plane of action to make money. You sure can't take it with you. Money isn't a good enough reason to do something unless we have a bigger plan, a higher purpose or intention for what it could do for us, our, families and the world.

Men give me credit for some genius. All the genius I have is this. When I have a subject in my mind, I study it profoundly. Day and night it is before me. My mind becomes pervaded with it…the effort which I have made is what people are pleased to call the fruit of genius. It is the fruit of labor and thought.

Alexander Hamilton, 1755-1804

The richness of your life and mine is not luck, not being born into the right family, and not being a mastermind. It is the fruit of our labor and our thought. Enjoy the fruits of your labors. My story is sweet, so is yours. Look closely and you will see what is there.

How are the fruits of your labor showing up? Spend time thinking about them in your own life. The fruits of your own labors are the sweetest because they are yours!

KEEP ON PLANTING! It is as simple as that.

I Can Do This Thing Called Wealth—and So Can YOU!

Mind Treatment: Infinite Supply

Step 1

The Universe, God, Spirit, Life is Infinite, all knowing and all powerful. IT is wealthy beyond measure. Whatever IT needs is there. Whatever is not there, IT calls into being from the formless. Infinite Supply is readily available to all.

Step 2

I live and am immersed in Infinite Intelligence. Just as God is wealthy beyond measure, so am I.

Step 3

Everything I need is right here where I am. If I can't see it, I call it into being. I thoroughly enjoy the richness of Life in me and around me. To be alive is a beautiful experience. I demonstrate plenty of money to live on, to play with and to share. I attract money to me like a magnet and I use it wisely and lovingly. Money is a perfect way for me to circulate in the world.

Step 4

I know that nothing or no one, especially myself, can get in the way of me living prosperously. Any old ideas about God or money are taken care of now and replaced with new expansive, empowering ones.

Step 5

I know that God, alone, is my Source and I appreciate all the many channels through which my good flows. I think rich, prosperous ideas about myself and my world.

Step 6

I am full of gratitude, appreciation and thanksgiving for all the riches I enjoy and for the great wealth that lies in me.

Step 7

I release this treatment knowing it continues to provide for me a rich, wonderful life. And so it is!

8
I Can Do This Thing Called Death

We need fear nothing in the Universe. We need not be afraid of God. We may be certain that all will arrive at the final goal that not one will be missing. Every man is an incarnation of God. The soul can no more be lost than God could be lost.

We believe in God and that He is Good. What more can life demand of us than that we do the best that we can and try to improve? If we have done this, we have done well and all will be right with our souls both here and hereafter. This leaves us free to work out our own salvation - not with fear or even with trembling - but with peace and in quiet confidence"

Ernest Holmes
Science of Mind, on Immortality

This chapter explores healthy, loving ways to look at death—both the constant death we undergo as part of our ongoing daily evolution and the finality of the life we are now living--in order to take away some of the fear, pain, and suffering around death.

People often come to their end, facing the unknown with dread, fighting to hold on with everything they got, believing that they will cease to exist once their body is gone. No one wants that. That idea surely feels wrong. No wonder many who are dying put up a fuss! There is much unnecessary drama. Those around them are limited in what they can do. They can either drug them or put up with it, supporting them the best way they can.

Most people have limited exposure to death, so they deny, fear or resist it by not thinking or talking about it. Much is misunderstood about the process and what it means. If we learn to look at it differently, we have an appreciation for what is going on.

In fact, death can be seen as a way of life. We are forever dying to something in order to give birth to something new. We need to get comfortable with it and learn to work alongside of it. Just as the snake is continuously shedding it's outermost layer, we, too, must always be in the process of letting go of that which no longer serves us, whether it be a body, a life, or a limiting idea.

There is no such thing as a final death or end. Rather, there's a change of form, a transition from one life to another. Most of the religious traditions and teachings believe in some kind of life after death. The story of Jesus tells of his return after the death of his body, proving to his disciples that there is no death, only life. The spirit lives.

Maybe you are not a religious person. Maybe you don't even think of yourself as spiritual. That's okay. Whoever we are and whatever we believe, if we look to nature, we find answers and clues to how life works.

Scientifically, energy cannot be destroyed. It merely changes from one form to another. When the dead animal on the side of the road decomposes, the body, made of energy, changes form. It disintegrates and goes back into the earth, providing nourishment for plant and animal life. This is part of the cycle of life. The life force, or spirit, of the animal has been released because the body is no longer functioning to support it. But that same energy that once animated the life form still exists somewhere.

There is a healthy, wholesome way to look at death and what it really is, no matter what you may have seen or experienced. Great gifts await our recognition. All we need to do is look for them. Is it possible for us to believe that whatever Spirit, which has kept us going throughout this lifetime has a plan for us in the afterlife? Even if this life has not been the experience we have hoped for or we have not been able to see the purpose of it all, is it possible for us to believe that there will come a time when we can see and appreciate the bigger picture of it all? If we have experienced any good at all here, can we believe that minimally, there will be some more good yet to come in the future for us?

There is no doubt a greater appreciation for life that comes when we are about to lose it. It is an amazing thing to be alive. Today we are at a place in consciousness where we can embrace the beauty of the passages we all have to face. When we look at death as a natural process that relieves and frees us, we can embrace our time and enjoy it for what it is: a natural progression of life. This is how Jesse, a member of our Center for Spiritual Living, handled her death.

Jesse's Gift

One of the greatest gifts I have ever received arrived early in my ministry, when Jesse, a member of our Center for Spiritual Living, called and asked to talk. She was in her early 70's and had just learned that she had leukemia. The prognosis wasn't good. When Jesse was told what the treatment would be, she decided to avoid a long, drawn-out, painful experience of death and asked me to help her end her life.

Jesse had enough. She knew herself, and under the circumstances, choosing to die sooner rather than later made sense to her. It was time to go.

I would be lying if I didn't say I was both shocked and surprised. As a brand new minister, this was my first experience with death, and Jesse looked quite young and capable to me. But I believe in people having the freedom to make choices that are right for them. I stayed calm and found the words I needed. I had never even heard of someone asking for help to go. I didn't even know it could be done. Thank God, our minister emeritus, Dr. Roy Graves, reminded me that I would always have what I needed. In every situation, whether I thought I knew or not, I would know what to say. Those words of wisdom came to me and I trusted they would carry me through.

Following the lead of my inner voice, I asked Jesse if there was anything left for her to do. With no hesitation, she replied that she wanted to have some special time with her son on his birthday, which would be soon. That seemed do-able. She then said jokingly that she also wanted to have a date with Robert Redford before she left. I had no idea how that was going to happen, and I certainly didn't know how this whole idea was going to play out. But I was just there to watch and learn--and of course, do my part: love and support her, know and trust a higher power was at work--and that was easy.

Pretty much playing it by ear, I encouraged Jesse to think about it some more before we talked again. Then we prayed together, affirming that it would all work out for her according to her desires. There was no question in my mind that since she had this idea, that she could go quickly and easily, there had to be a way for her to do so. Otherwise, she could not have had the idea in the first place. The Universe, Infinite Intelligence, works perfectly, and our desires are signals to us that there is a way available to us to have them fulfilled.

A few weeks later, we were having a church picnic and Jesse arrived late with her daughter. She whispered to me that she had her date with Robert. I couldn't wait to hear this one.

As it happened, a new movie with Robert Redford had just come out, and her daughter had taken her to see it that day. Jesse was perfectly satisfied with enjoying him in a movie. That was her date. It worked for her, and if it worked for her, it worked for me. I had to give it to the Universe; good job, Universe! Who would have ever thought of that? Not me. Very creative.

Next, Jesse had her day in the park with her son, celebrating his birthday. That was their last time together. Afterwards, she came home and went to bed, happy to be complete with her life.

Late the following morning, Jesse's daughter called to tell me that she had found her mother still asleep. Respecting her mother's wishes, she let her be, not knowing what to do next. Again, following Spirit's lead, I said that I would be over shortly.

When I arrived, Jesse was in an undisturbed sleep. Sitting next to her, I laid my hand on her back and went into prayer. I treated my own mind about Jesse by celebrating her life, her freedom. Within hours she was gone.

Wow! It could be done. Someone could set the intention to leave, and go within a very short amount of time. This was a powerful experience for me, and for Jesse's family, too. The timing was incredible. It did not take place until Jesse felt she had done everything she wanted to do here, and when her list was complete, she was gone. The process was fascinating. I stood in awe of how beautifully the Universe works.

Jesse is one of the greatest teachers I have ever had. She taught me that whether to live or die is our choice, and that we can have it any way we want. When Jesse died, everything was in order. She had lived a full, rich life, and had felt complete.

This is how Jesse approached death:

She knew she was more than her body.

She knew she was more than her life experience.

She knew she was spirit.

She bypassed the disease she chose not to have, refusing to put herself and her family through what she believed was unnecessary pain and suffering.

She transcended a long, drawn out, painful death; she got what she needed to know without going through suffering.

She knew herself and what was best for her.

She was at a point in her life where this made sense to her.

She maintained her personal power through it all.

She directed the show.

Jesse died an honorable death. It was her creation. I was just there to support her through it. The Intelligence in her body listened and responded. God, Intelligence, Spirit, in her made it so. It was a beautiful to be with her on this journey, and watch and learn I did. I will always be grateful to her for including me in the sacred transition from one life to another. This very special teacher made it possible for me to help many others move through their transitions with grace and ease.

Life is Always a Choice

My father, who died suddenly and unexpectedly--and then paradoxically lived for many long years after he died--also contributed to my education. He demonstrated that for everyone involved, there's something perfect about a death.

A firefighter for the City of Milwaukee, my dad first died in the early morning hours of Labor Day, in the early 80's, while fighting a fire in an old scrap paper company.

When it was clear that the building couldn't be saved and the order to leave was issued, it was too late for my father: the floor gave way beneath him, and he was buried under bales of paper.

By the time dad was uncovered, he was no longer breathing, and his co-workers and friends worked hard to bring him back to life. Though they knew there was a risk that he had been without oxygen for too long and had suffered brain damage, they didn't know what else to do. They wanted him to live and they did everything they could. We all believed they did the right thing.

We were horrified when the doctors told us it was a mistake for him to live. Brain damage was certain and the quality of his life would never be the same. Weeks later, they disconnected him from life support, and he was able to breathe on his own. That was all the encouragement we needed to believe there was hope that he was making progress.

At the time, we had no idea that he was to be in a coma for the next 13 years.

It was a very dark time for my family and all who knew us. We were all shaken to the core. For days, my mother couldn't even pick up one of the three new babies that were born into the family that year. This was not the way we thought it all would go. We were supposed to have dad until he was old. He had been so active and youthful. Even in his early 50's he could keep up with those much younger. Joy was knocked out of us all. Within two years of his accident, my whole life fell apart.

My mother eventually brought dad home and was able to care for him with the help of visiting nurses who came in daily to help out. He was paralyzed, and they got him out of bed and into a wheel chair twice a day. He could look at us, but there was no expression on his face. All he could do was cough or groan if he wasn't comfortable. We had no idea what he was thinking or feeling.

Dad was the love of mom's life, and she continued to include him in everything as she always had done. Everyone, including the smallest grandchild, talked to him and felt very comfortable having him there. Most of the grandchildren hadn't even known him before the accident.

Near the end of dad's life--when it was clear that all of mom's praying wasn't going to bring about a miracle that would change his state--she became restless, and traveled whenever she had the opportunity. Who could blame her? When the accident occurred, she had been in her early 50's, a young woman in her prime, younger than I am now.

In time, like my mother, I began to recover from my divorce and make a new life for myself, which included becoming a minister. As areas of my life healed, I was free to expand my focus, I wondered: Why is dad still here? For what purpose?

The answer came while I was in Whitefish, Montana at a ministers' conference. I had some time to myself, and while sitting at the foothills of the stunning Glacier National Park, it came to me that my father was staying for my mother. He was hanging on because she wasn't ready to let him go, and regardless of being in a coma, he was still committed to his family.

Shortly after this realization, I was in town visiting and had a chance to watch dad one afternoon when no one else was around. This was rare because the family home was normally like Grand Central Station.

Considering that more health issues had begun to emerge for my father, and that my mother was getting involved in a new life, it came to me to say, "Dad, you have done such a great job. If you need to go, we understand. Mom will be all right. We will, too."

For the first time in 13 years, I had evidence that he heard me: I saw a tear rolling down his cheek. Two weeks later, I got a call that he wasn't doing well and they started him on morphine. I knew this was the end. I cried all day. We were losing him a second time.

Thinking that a walk around the beautiful greens would ease my grief, John and I attended a Women's Golf Tournament in Orlando, where we live. Though it was a gorgeous January day in Florida and I was surrounded by so much beauty, I was miserable and had a hard time keeping it together.

I called home early in the afternoon and clearly the time had come. In the midst of my sorrow and grief, it dawned on me that I was crying for myself, for my loss, and that I wasn't really thinking of dad and his process. I changed my focus to him and his release. This helped me immensely. Late that afternoon, he was gone.

Through the years I have been blessed by many dreams of dad—or perhaps, visits with him. He is always his happy, youthful, healthy self. I also hear his voice every time I make peanut butter sandwiches. To this day, he cautions me that using too much peanut butter makes it hard for the kids to eat the sandwich. At other times, dad reassures me that he continues to live and we are still connected. These experiences bring me great peace and comfort. I know that my dad is still part of my life.

Life is always a choice, even if we're in a coma.

Way to Go

Recently, I broke a glass that shattered everywhere in our new kitchen. Tile floors can be very unforgiving. It was the end of a long, demanding day. I said to John, "Please remind me that when I am tired, I need to get out of the kitchen." The same can be said as to how one lives. There is a time to get out of Life's way and move on to greater things.

There are other options to death than waiting to be done unto by sickness, disease, or accidents, waiting until we finally run out of gas, or are taken by the Universe, Spirit, God at our appointed time.

Suicide is of course an option though taking one's life doesn't seem very natural, because it's usually an unhappiness or dire situation that brings someone to that point. There is definitely a lot of negative energy associated with suicide, especially for those left behind. Hearing that a person has taken their life in that way helps us to see that there are other more peaceful, loving ways to go. It helps us to get clear about how we want to live and how we want to die. For example, I have decided not to leave in order to get out of some problem or something that is "happening to me." I would rather be fully complete and satisfied with my experience here, be on good terms with my loved ones, and leave them in the best of possible conditions.

Joseph Murphy, metaphysical teacher and author, "had it down". He knew how to bring closure to his life. He and his wife were well traveled, had money, enjoyed life--did what they wanted. Shortly after another trip around the world, he decided it was time for him to leave. Even though he was in perfect health, he was eager to move on. He told his wife he wanted to go peacefully. He called his closest friends to share his decision with them, thanking them and wishing them the best. He then lay down to sleep, never to wake up again. It can be that easy. It can also be meaningful. He died with dignity and honor.

The Australian Aborigines were said to know how to leave their bodies in the sand and enter the next dimension. They made a conscious choice when they believed it was time to leave. They had a big celebration, went apart, sat in the sand, closed their eyes to this world, and within minutes, were gone.

There is an art to knowing when and how to go. Our choice is by design or default. I know that some may have a problem with that kind of thinking, believing that the time of death is God's decision. But if we believe instead that we are in a close, intimate partnership with God, then we will be working together on the hour of our death and it will be divine right timing and a more gentle, peaceful exit.

Stay Connected

It's essential to live our own lives and take care of ourselves, no matter what's going on with those around us, especially if they are making their transition and live in the same house. I'm not saying it's a good idea to ignore them. I'm not saying they have to go it alone. I'm just saying that some of these transition processes take years: for my father, it was thirteen, and for my mother, it was three. I'm just saying that life goes on, and that it's not healthy to drop everything in order to be there for our loved one 24/7.

Of course, in the final days we want to be close. But in the meantime, we need to ask for help. We need to leave the house, take a walk, work out, go to church or a spiritual center, go out for lunch with a friend, treat ourselves well. Months before my mother passed, a week-long retreat in the Canadian Rockies helped prepare me. The Universe gave me the love and support I needed to be fully present for what was to come.

In a way, I had it easy because my family and I lived eight hours away from my mother. We didn't have to deal with things up close and personal, as family members who lived near mom did. On the other hand, I never knew exactly what was going on. The news was always delayed, and by the time I rushed home in response to an "emergency," mom was feeling good again. I'd arrive mourning her impending death and wanting to connect with her, and she'd be getting ready for dinner, going shopping, or out to see a movie. She wanted no pity. Most days, she'd say, "It's not so bad." I found myself wondering why I felt sorry for her. I guess I felt sorry for myself. What would life be like without her?

As mom's life drew to an end, she continued to have very good days-- after a blood transfusion--and very bad days--when she was due for a transfusion. We spent so much time going up and down with her on an emotional roller coaster that it was difficult to focus on our own lives. Considering how difficult it must have been for her, she made the most of it. She had tricked her sister and the DMV into renewing her driver's license, and insisted on driving herself whenever she wanted to go out. We couldn't get her to see how dangerous this was, for both herself and others, and secretly spoke of disabling her car in some way, though it never came to that.

At one particularly difficult point, I decided to stop asking myself "What's happening to my little mommy?" and instead, to be happy for her. For my own sanity, I vowed to hold a vision of the bigger picture, even when mom was denying what was happening. Reminding myself that she believed in heaven made all the difference for me. How could heaven be so bad? I also began working on this book during this time, and that, too, helped keep me emotionally balanced.

Never knowing when she was in need of a blood transfusion until it was upon her, affected her mind and how she was thinking. I like to believe, and in fact, I do believe, that in preserving my sanity, I was a bigger help to my mom and the rest of the family. During my last visit with her, her house was clean, bright, and cheerful. There was no evidence of sickness anywhere. She loved games, and played cards and board games with the family. In her last days, she even taught us a new game.

It's so easy to fall into a hole and stop living our own life when a family member has been diagnosed as terminally ill. It can be such a distraction, can keep us from what we really need to do for ourselves-- especially if it's our mother or father who is dying. But even then, we don't have to be caught up in the drama 24 hours a day. We all have a path to follow, and it's up to us to stick to our own path. The loved one can still have our attention. We can be loving and supportive—especially if we take care of ourselves and keep our head about us.

As Time Draws Near

It was late October when it became clear that my mom's final hours were fast approaching. There were signs. For example, when I phoned her during one of her stays at the hospital, she made a big deal about the clock on the wall falling down. I thought that metaphysically, this may mean her time was up. She also said that she saw my dad sitting in the bed next to her and wondered what he was doing there. Shortly after making these bizarre comments, she returned home, and once again, things took a turn for the worse: she developed an infection in her leg.

In another phone conversation, mom sounded fine as we discussed plans for Thanksgiving. But then she fell one night, and my aunt couldn't lift her. My brother, who lived two doors down, rushed to the rescue, and as he picked mom up, she told him that she was ready to go. That was it. I knew it was time.

John was out of town, so after taking care of business, I collected Joseph from school and hurried home. We didn't know how long we'd be gone or what we might need so we packed all evening, planning to leave early the next morning. But that night, our new alarm system came on and I couldn't shut it off. Hours later, someone from the alarm company finally took care of it and Joseph and I we went to bed, exhausted. Then, around 4:00 a.m., an owl hooting in our backyard woke me up. Though we hadn't planned to leave quite that early, there was no way I was going to ignore the warnings. They were loud and clear! It was time to go. We packed the car and headed north.

Fortunately, there was still time to give my mother a fond farewell. One evening a few days before she made her transition, my mother's five children, all but one of their spouses and some of the grandchildren, stood around her bed and thanked her individually for gifts she had given them and what those gifts meant to them. We had a chance to send her off with wishes for courage, improvement, health, well-being, and love. This was a great healing experience for my family. A portal of love opened and we felt the outpouring of love envelope us. We felt supported through the process. It was good to be together.

I am so grateful to have witnessed the stages of my mother's transition. The focus of her consciousness detached from the outer and turned inward, and as her world shrank, she became less involved with what was going on, and more quiet. Gradually, she became less conscious, staring off into space. And, she slept more, until that is all she did.

When I spoke of my hope to be by my mother's bedside at the moment of her death, the social worker that was there to support us cautioned me that very private people usually don't want anyone around when they go. That would be my mom. After five nights of vigil, we were exhausted, and a Hospice worker took over, sitting with her all night. The first time the sitter left the room for a brief period, my mom was out of there. She had, indeed, wanted to be alone.

How will you know when it's time? Watch for signs that will surely be there. Listen carefully and follow your inner guidance.

Rule No. 48

I can blame it on Aunt Betty, my mom's only sister, but it didn't take me long to join in. My mother had a wardrobe to die for (interesting choice of words there), and less than 48 hours after her death, we were trying on her clothes. I know what you're going to say, because I never thought I'd be one of those people who just couldn't wait to get the casket closed to start dividing up the stuff. I am a minister. I should know better.

I could have, perhaps should have, waited at least 48 hours. But we would only be there for a few more days, and I chose to jump into fun. It seemed cathartic, somehow. After watching mom in pain and agony for so long, it was time to blow off some steam. Since we weren't into heavy drinking as her ancestors may have been while having a party around the dead body sitting in the middle of the room we needed some release, and this seemed the perfect thing to do. We had a fashion show together. Every now and then, we would go out and share something with John, who was watching TV in the living room. I am sure he really wondered about us, but he was kind and loving enough not to kill the moment. Knowing that there were three memorials to face--one in Columbia, South Carolina, where mom had died; another in Milwaukee, where she would be buried next to my father; and the last in her hometown of St. Louis, with family and friends--we needed to play.

I have heard that our loved ones linger after their death. I couldn't help but wonder what mom thought of our "fashion show," and if I would regret it forever. Now I believe she enjoyed it. Maybe she gave us the idea to begin with. Anyway, she was happy now. She was free and so were we and . . . I forgave myself.

We Do Our Best

I understand that some of my statements regarding death may sound glib. Being a part of death stirs things up for us emotionally, whether it's happening to us as we transition into greater versions of ourselves, or to a loved one who is transitioning completely out of this world and into the next. Often, there is pain, suffering, and sadness as we adjust to what's going on and prepare for what the end result will mean to us. Losing a loved one rips our hearts apart, and we may temporarily feel as though we ourselves have died. This is evidence that we truly are connected to one another in the great web of Life.

As I write this chapter, our cat Spikey has made his transition. I am reminded that on the human level we get quite attached to other beings. I have never had a pet before, so this has been a new death experience for

138

me. So many feelings came up for both my son, Joseph, and me. Spikey was Joseph's buddy. They grew up together.

It's hard for all of us not to miss Spikey's big, beautiful eyes staring right through to our soul. He represented that pure, unconditional love that we tend to lose sight of in ourselves and others. His presence was a reminder of a more peaceful, meditative, loving way to live. He was a reflection of our inner, authentic selves, that part of us that's pure and perfect. Now we must remember who we are on our own, and behave accordingly.

Often, it's our own unfinished business that comes up during a loss. We regret those times when we could have been more patient or loved more unconditionally. We regret having missed some of the cues and signals of what our loved one really needed, or we regret things we wish we had said.

Life here isn't always easy. Sometimes we're far too busy for our own good. We take on more responsibilities than we can honestly uphold, and being in relationship with people or animals requires us to be present and to give to them fully. After all, how many eggs can you carry in your life's basket before they start to crack? We may be perfect spirits, but the truth is that as evolving souls in the human form, we're never done. We're always perfectly unfolding, so we must forgive ourselves for where we are and keep on going, with the intention of using what we learn in a more meaningful way as we go.

There are going to be things we could have done better, and things that others could do better regarding us. It's easy to see all that when it's over. We do our best, and then we need to let it go.

The more honest we are with ourselves about our joys, pains, misgivings, and all that's involved with them, the more we find relief.

Becoming morbid, thinking of all the ways we failed, beating ourselves up, doesn't help. What does help is to feel our emotions and allow ourselves to grieve. The fastest way to get through an uncomfortable feeling such as a loss is to embrace it, and move into the pain, instead of denying or resisting it. So take time out for yourself, let yourself *be*. Allow yourself to cry. Surround yourself with others who understand. For myself, being with family members and friends who are experiencing the same thing has always brought comfort.

Unresolved feelings that are buried intensify and surface later in unexpected ways that are damaging to our health. They continue to require a part of our energy, leaving less for the business of living fully in the moment. But if we allow ourselves to grieve properly, we can make peace with the death and prepare to go on with our lives, making the adjustments and changes that are in order. Sad moments can be expected with the loss of someone we were very close to. We can take comfort in knowing that there will always be a place for them in our hearts.

As we courageously face the situations and circumstances that trigger our emotions, we feel freer.

As we focus on the good things we shared and appreciate how much we have grown through our experiences together, we feel better.

As we forgive ourselves and each other for the difficult times, we feel relief.

Each person is responsible for their own life. That means we are making our own decisions every step of the way. For however long we travel on a similar path side by side, we are grateful. We appreciate whatever time we had because we know that life is fragile and temporary, that our time is limited.

If we believe that Life is good and that it is for us, we can know that there was perfection in what we shared together. At heart level we have left an impression upon each other. Because of our time together, we are not the same. We touched each other deeply, and we changed for the better.

This is the way to healing: Be gentle and kind to yourself. You did better than you thought. Love heals all. Even our pets have a choice as to whether to stay or to go. I have to believe that Spikey, also being an eternal being and continuously expanding, got what he came here for and gave us what he had to share with us. For that, we are so grateful.

It's Personal

Dr. Kennedy Schultz, my teacher, was abandoned by his mother at birth when she died. Under difficult conditions, and extreme poverty, his father did his best to support the children. In spite of this challenging background, my teacher created a nice life for himself.

As a minister for over twenty years, Dr. Schultz shared what he knew with others so that they, too, could experience a wonderful new life. A father figure to his students, he taught us everything he knew about the Science of Mind: how to think and how to live. He gave us back to ourselves, and literally transformed many who truly had been victimized and whose lives seemed to be over. We all thought the world of him.

Less than a year after his retirement party, we were horrified to learn that Dr. Schultz had a brain tumor. How could this happen, with everything he knew? What chance did we have if even he did not get it "right" in the end? We were devastated. It seemed such a tragic end for this man who loved so greatly.

Through the passage of time, I have come to believe that though my teacher was extremely accomplished, he too had some other things to learn before he left: This was his time to be loved and taken care of.

I have no idea what he did actually learn from the experience. I do know it had to be perfect for him, and while it looked messy, even ugly, to all those close to him, I believe that it was really good between him and his maker. And though—or perhaps because--he was virtually helpless at the physical level, he gave us all a great gift: permission to take our focus off of how things look from the outside and put our attention on getting what we came here for--whatever that may be to us.

Death is a personal matter. We may speculate all we want about someone's life and death, and yet we will never know what really went down in the end. That's between the one who dies and God.

Always Connected (Together)

When I was still a new minister, I received a call from a friend whose brother had just died in a plane crash. She wanted me to come and talk with her family, especially her mother, who was having a really difficult time. The funeral had already taken place in their Catholic Church with friends and family, so I was surprised and honored that I was asked to come.

I had to feel my way through this one, as I did with Jesse, and once again, I was perfectly guided. We talked. I asked questions about what had happened, about what my friend's brother had been like, and as we got closer to the family's emotions, their pain began to surface.

My friend said, "If only I could have talked to him one more time, I would feel better. I don't feel complete about this. It all happened so fast. I never got to say goodbye." Just as I had known that there had to be a

141

way for Jesse to die as she wished, I knew that there had to be a way for my friend to complete this unfinished business. If there was no way, then she wouldn't have the desire.

So we prayed, affirming that the way would be shown and that all involved were lovingly supported in their loss.

After a month or so, I received a thank you note from my friend saying that it was all taken care of. She had gotten her wish. Curious, I called to find out more. She said she'd had the most fabulous dream of being with her brother. In the dream, he was whole, and they sat together and expressed their feelings for each other. When they both had expressed all they needed to, he walked up some stairs and was gone. She was happy. She could now move on. Case closed.

Dreams can be so healing. Two weeks after my mother's transition, I woke up realizing that I had just had an encounter with her as I slept. In a dream, I was in a huge family room. There were lots of people I seemed to know all around me.

All of a sudden I looked up and my mother was there. She led me to a quiet room in the back of the huge house. Aware that she was gone from this life, I was surprised to see her, especially because in the dream, she was healthy, happy, and vibrant. I could feel her energy. She looked great. I remember thinking how different she was. She had never been an overly affectionate person, but in the dream, she wanted to be close. I felt strange but good in her presence, happy to just *be* with her. It seemed so natural.

Then, I saw a bed with messy covers on it and asked her if she had slept with so much going on all night in the living room. She said, "Yes, I slept."

Some would dismiss this as just a dream. But dreams have great power, and this one brought me a message that I will never forget: My mother is awake, and whatever transition period she was in when I dreamt of her, she was more herself than ever. This made it much easier for me to go on without her physically being here. Thank you God. I had been waiting for that.

Celebration of Life

Many believe that we have to get sick to die, and that if we don't fight for our lives, they will be taken away from us. Still others believe that suffering is necessary preparation for heaven and many don't think much about death until it appears at their own door or that of their families.

These wrong ideas about death are happening all around us because people are walking asleep though their lives, oblivious to what is really going on, distracted in busyness, entertainment, and confusion. They don't know any better. The more quickly we can have a greater understanding of how Life works and our relationship with IT, the better for us all. There are a lot of things we can do as individuals to make the world a better place, especially regarding how to live and how to die.

When we believe that we must get sick to die, we will get sick to die. When we believe we have to fight for our lives, we will have to fight for our lives. When we believe we have to suffer in order to be worthy of entering the pearly white gates of heaven, we will suffer. Many believe these things about death because it's how others who have gone before them have died. But it doesn't have to be this way unless we believe it does.

The true Reality of Life is that we can have it any way we want. We get to choose how it will be.

If we know there is no death and that life goes on, is it possible for us to enjoy the way of things? Is it possible for us to stop the doom and gloom, bring more light and love to the end of this segment of our never-ending lives? I believe that as we grow and mature, have a healthier more wholesome relationship with ourselves and those we are involved with, especially Spirit, it will become easier and easier.

One day, without all the drama separating us from loved ones, we may even give up death altogether. It's conceivable that as we raise our vibrations, this form (body) we are currently using will renew right where we are. Still, at this point in our evolution, it often times seems a blessing when someone passes on especially if there is pain and suffering involved.

In any case, passages, transitions, deaths are all a part of life. Even messy ones are good. They serve their purpose, and a life that ends without a physical healing is not necessarily a failure, as long as the soul gets what they came here to get. It really is always between us and God, Spirit, the Universe. No one else needs to know or understand. Things may not always be what they appear to be.

Of one thing we can be sure: Death is always greater than it looks. Behind the scenes, great work is being accomplished. We don't always get what we want, but we always get what we need, and what we need most of all is for our souls to accomplish what they came here for.

In a very real sense, we are continuously dying to our old self and being born to our new self. These are sacred, reflective times that allow us to get in touch with who we are. As we learn to celebrate these deaths, large and small, and see them for what they are, we become more comfortable with them. We are able to enjoy the truly remarkable experiences that are there for us to participate in and learn from.

Great gifts are waiting for us, and whatever death process you may be going through is an opportunity to release what no longer serves you and make room for the new.

As we give up thoughts of "poor me" or having been defeated, and stop asking questions like: "How could this happen to me, or why?" we open ourselves up to what is next. Glimpses of new possibility come, its easier for us to see that what went before was good and had meaning. It was all preparation for what was yet to be. Perfection was and is at work with us all.

The more quickly we move through our own process, the better we will feel. Greater possibilities than we ever considered are waiting to be born in us. When all of the stuck, limited, unhealthy energy is finally unblocked, our spirits are free to soar. We will get a view of a new life for ourselves. Life is forever waiting to be born in us anew.

And so we prepare not to die, but to live. The thought of death should slip from our consciousness altogether; and when this great event of the soul takes place, it should be beautiful, sublime . . . a glorious experience. As the eagle, freed from its cage, soars to its native heights, so the soul, freed from the home of heavy flesh, will rise and return unto its Father's house, naked and unafraid.

Ernest Holmes,
Science of Mind

"I Can Do This Thing Called Death -- And So Can YOU!"

Mind Treatment – Perfect Transitions

Step 1

There is only One Life and that is the Life of Spirit.

Step 2

That Life is my Life too. I am a part of IT.

Step 3

I am an infinite being. I go beyond the life I am currently living. I am forever growing and expanding, which means I am forever transitioning from old to new.

Step 4

I release all worries and concerns about dying to the old and being born to the new, whether it be through small changes and shifts that I experience in this life or in my more significant transition to the next.

Step 5

Whatever losses I appear to face are overcome by my greater good. With every transition, I feel more alive and more myself. Even though I am always free, I feel even freer.

Step 6

I appreciate my new, positive, healthy outlook on life changes and transition. I am so grateful to be alive. I enjoy my time wherever I am, immensely. I am grateful to be a part of the grand unfoldment of Life, as me.

Step 7

As I release this treatment, it continues to enliven me to all Life has to offer.

And so it is!

9
The Great "AH HA"

Undoubtedly we are surrounded by, and immersed in, a perfect Life: a complete, normal, happy, sane, harmonious and peaceful existence. But only as much of this Life as we embody will really become ours to use.

Ernest Holmes
Science of Mind

One of the best "ah ha" moments came to me while I was trying to have a baby in my early 40's. There are times when you absolutely cannot miss the Truth. The idea of having a baby was coming through me so strong. Even though I had two children from an earlier life, I missed much of their younger years growing up because we were physically separated. I compensated by being as available as I could by phone. Still, it was not the whole experience. There was something incomplete about the way things went, something not quite finished for me.

Beyond the obvious reasons of age, I was so much more aware now than I was in my twenties when I first had babies. I had more fears and doubts than I did then, but I believed my body could do it. That wasn't the problem. Women were proving that. There were also plenty of women having problems getting pregnant like I was. It seems today we have lost our connection with nature. Therefore we lose confidence and trust in our own natural abilities and instead give away our power to every little thing that could possibly go wrong.

Even though I knew better, intellectually, I was no different than anyone else. Discussions about the use of hair dye, microwaves, chemicals in lipstick, diet sodas, pesticides and more were my triggers. Underneath all that was the fear of opening my heart up again to a new little being. Pain left from my first round of having children and all that transpired was still there and it wasn't just memories of labor. Those are easy to forget. There were layers to unfold.

So while I said I wanted another baby and thought it would be a great experience for John and me, especially because he never had a child, neither of us had any idea what kind of adventure we were embarking upon.

With each miscarriage, of which there were three, I felt closer to where I needed to be. Each time, I found myself having to go deeper still. There were definite things that came up for me to work on. One day, my doctor called me into her office and asked, "What's up? Do you really want to have this baby? " I felt she was intuitively picking up on my underlying conflict. I said, "Yes I really do want this baby and I am working on some things, personally, about it." I was not about to go into everything with her as well intentioned as she was. I knew I was getting close. I could feel it.

So, much of this time, I insisted on working this out myself. Staunch independence and self-reliance can work against you. My teacher, Dr. Kennedy Shultz, after hearing of my troubles said, "I can't help you if I don't know what's going on". It was time to open up.

In a letter he wrote,

As far as the miscarriage is concerned, I wouldn't psychologize yourself to death over it. It leads into duality, and that is what we are so diligent about teaching people to move away from. There is no one keeping score on your life and deciding whether or not you deserve to have another child. If this were the way the law worked, child bearing on this planet would have come to a halt a long time ago. I think your treatment needs to be designed to create a mental equivalent of yourself and John as loving people eager to make a commitment to let a child come into this world and live beautifully by means of your love, and your wisdom. You both have done much to develop that love and wisdom, and you want to use it now creatively in all things. IT IS THAT SIMPLE! Remember, the Law doesn't know "deserve" it only knows "desire" backed up by "belief" in the rightness of the desire.

Months later, he emailed me a mind treatment:

I realize that the unfailing Creator of all that can be, moving creatively through my open mind and heart, has made me an ideal mother to my children, and a perfect prospect for bringing new life into the world as a new and beautiful child.

As the womb of my consciousness is alight with pure vitality and clear understanding, the womb of my body is a warm and nurturing and beautifully functioning place. It is a fitting place for a new life to begin and a safe place for a new life to take form.

The radiance of this right recognition of me as ideal mother shines through all negative experience. It is the real and the only creative power at work in my life. I accept it. I recognize it. And I let it be so. And so it is!

Each time I read it, I felt my confidence was building. I got pregnant again. When I started to fret and worry, I reminded myself that all I needed was the faith of a mustard seed. That wasn't so much. John and I started playing with names. We decided that if it was a girl, we would call her Emmalee, a boy would be Joseph. John always knew that if he had a son, his name would be Joseph. It didn't matter that we already had two Joes on my side of the family. I let it go as I had my pick of names with my first two, (Nicholas and Elizabeth) and I always liked the name Joseph.

One Sunday morning after our Sunday Celebration, I walked into the Youth room to teach a class and found a lone colored picture on the table with the name Emmalee on it. As far as I could remember that day, there were not any new children, especially any new little girls. I picked it up and put it in my briefcase and forgot about it. I did some inquiry and no one seemed to know anything about an Emmalee.

Early that week, I was going through my briefcase and ran across this big blue egg coloring with the name, Emmalee, on it. I couldn't help but think about it. It was so strange. I began to feel something opening up in me that I hadn't realized was closed. It was almost like this was a personal message to me from God, or Emmalee. All of a sudden she became real to me. She had my attention.

Later that same day, I was preparing to teach a class and began reading about the nature of God and what IT does by Ernest Holmes in the *Science of Mind* textbook. This is what I read:

Here and now, we are surrounded by, and immersed in, an Infinite Good. How much of this Infinite Good is ours? ALL OF IT! And how much of IT may we have to use? AS MUCH OF IT AS WE CAN EMBODY.

I finally put two and two together and got it. I connected the dots. I had not embodied, emotionally, a baby. I cried. I had not let myself get totally wrapped up in the idea of a new child in my life. I was holding back. The brakes were on for me, not with God. I wasn't allowing myself to think about it too much just in case it didn't happen. I didn't let myself get involved, emotionally, with the idea, for fear that I would get hurt again or never really get to experience my desire.

I longed to experience the fulfillment of my heart's desire. We all do. I was terrified that I would be denied the opportunity again. We all know what that feels like. I had been working on myself, intellectually, and I hadn't taken it far enough. The closed part of my heart had to open up and be vulnerable before I could demonstrate, and when it opened, everything fell into place.

I will never forget that realization. It was one of those things you can't know until you, personally, have one. Kind of like, in the early years of having sex, I was told I wasn't having orgasms. I didn't know what an orgasm was, or even that I was supposed to be having one until I finally did. In this case, I had thought I was open to my greater good, which was having a baby. And then, I felt what an opening really was. My heart stretched open wider than ever. I was flooded with emotions without really understanding all that was going on.

I never could have orchestrated what happened…two different things grabbing my attention, love and letting go of fear, and then, coming together as a realization. That is what the Universe does. IT will find a way to get us unstuck and open us up. IT will even take us beyond where we think we want to go.

This was something that wanted and needed to happen as a part of my spiritual journey. I thought I wanted a baby, which really was a form. The desire behind that form was my desire to be healed and returned to wholeness, even if I couldn't see that. If it hadn't happened with a pregnancy, because I had decided this was my last try, it would have come about in another way because this was something that needed to take place in me. Obviously, an Emmalee didn't appear but she did play her part. Interestingly, the art piece drawn was of *blue* egg. Joseph happened. Maybe Joseph is Emmalee turned boy. Maybe John needed to experience a son. Who knows? God does.

The Thing ITself will find a way and always give us more than we expected. A beautiful boy came into our life. My heart was opened. I was able to be more fully present to my older children, and give to them in better ways with all the new concepts I was learning. A much greater love has allowed *our* relationships to make up for lost time, and go beyond what we ever thought was possible.

"I fully trust and embody my true heart's desires knowing they are already mine."

"I Can Do This Thing Called Life and So Can YOU!"

10
You Are Created for Greatness

You are already a success at manifesting and using the creative principle. Anytime you demonstrate the same thing over and over again in your life, you can say you are successful in demonstrating that particular thing. It may not be what you want. Even if you are creating it, there may just be some adjustments that need to be made in order to get more of what you want.

You may have a long history of ill-health or bad finances. You have been successful in creating that, and in keeping it going as your experience even if it isn't what you want. By the very fact that you can make that kind of thing happen, you are successful. What you believe and whatever it is that you keep doing, keeps whatever it is going for you in your life. Whatever that is, you have it down to a T. It's natural and easy for you. Would you agree?

Of course that isn't good enough. It's not even acceptable when you could be experiencing so much more. Why settle? There are no brownie points for doing without or accepting less. When you make the connection between what you are attracting into your life experience and what you believe, you will see the part you have played in the whole thing, because our thoughts and beliefs create our experience. It's important for us to see that we are first cause to what goes on. When we see the part we have played in the creation of something, we can learn to change our thoughts and beliefs to create a more desirable outcome. The success element is a part of your nature. Celebrate the fact that it is natural and easy for you to be a success.

What are you deciding to be successful about?

Is it what you want?

Does it support you? If not, it is purely a matter of redirecting what you are doing, saying and being, to something which supports the idea of what you would like to see and experience.

Hosea 1:10 says, "You are sons of the living God." God created us out of ITself. Being ALL, there is nothing else IT could have created us

151

out of. Is God good? Of course God is good. That means you are good, too, no matter what anyone says.

Dr. Holmes in *This Thing Called You* wrote,

Then the thing you are after is already here, within you. The only things that stand between you and it are the accumulated thoughts, beliefs and emotions of the ages. But there is nothing, there, that has not been put there either by yourself or the human race. What has been put there can be removed...Your job is to reject them.

Your job is to be more and more conscious of what you accept as truth, to question your thoughts and beliefs, reject what no longer applies and accept new, larger ideas for yourself. The interesting thing is that the moment you start cleaning out and tossing the old, the new rises to the surface. Why? It was there all along. Just because you couldn't see it, doesn't mean it wasn't there. It was always just below the surface.

You were born with everything you could ever possibly need or want. The gift has already been given. Wisdom is already your nature. Love is who you are. Peace is at the heart of your being. YES, YOU CAN DO THIS THING CALLED LIFE because you were hardwired with everything you could possibly need to be a success!

If you really want to do something, you can. You may have to give up the fight and struggle. Who are you fighting anyway? After all is said and done the only real fight is with yourself. You may think it is with your significant other, your family or the people you work with. Ultimately, when we are frustrated or mad, it is with ourselves for something we have allowed or done. Maybe we did something for the wrong reason or because we felt pressured by those around us.

There is no need to prove ourselves. There is no ill-feeling we cannot overcome. Whatever it may be, when we discover who we really are, we know we are already good. Then we can get on with the business of loving ourselves and others and creating richer, more meaningful lives.

Raymond Charles Barker, wrote in *Science of Successful Living*,

The natural man is a spiritual potential. Left alone he will not go to his doom but will progress, evolve rapidly and bring forth a better world than he ever knew before. Man is essentially good. The evil characteristics of the human mind and emotions are merely the left-overs from his trail of evolution.

How freeing is it to know that?

Are you ready to get rid of your left-over thoughts and beliefs? You and I are spiritual potential. We have great potential to be more and live well. What we hold in our minds and hearts is more precious than anything we possess. Expansive, abundant, loving and wise thoughts are our first priority. The more impressed we are with thoughts of good than ones of worry or concern about what is going on around us, the greater the quality of our lives. Our lives will literally transform before our eyes.

The human self can only take things so far. We dance around the edges of a very inviting, beautiful, immense pool of water. Sooner or later we have to jump in and let go of control and experience the wonder and joy of Life. That's taking it to the next level.

Things don't really start getting good in life until we are ready to open up our hearts to God. Our problems are related to the nature of our relationship with the Infinite. Our beliefs about IT play an important part in our understanding of Life and how IT works. We can't help be in relationship at all times because we live and move and have our being in God. Sometimes we forget and this feels like we are separated and alone. Even when we remember, is it possible for us to really see what kind of relationship we have? Are we having a real, live, active, intimate relationship with our Source? Are we enjoying as much life as there is for us to enjoy?

We are on a journey that goes on forever. There will always be more for us to be conscious of. Something inside of us knows we were created for more. There is that within us that resonates with a Truth when we hear it. We know when we know.

"I was created for greatness and so were you!"

"I Can Do This Thing Called Life and So Can YOU!"

Part 3
Spiritual Practices

11
Everything's A Practice

What is a practice? A practice is something we agree to do on a consistent and regular basis in order to improve our performance. A spiritual practice is something we agree to do on a consistent basis so that we can live our life from a more spiritually aware place that is satisfying, fulfilling, and successful. A practice keeps us open, and receptive for divine guidance and inspiration. It keeps us connected in a busy world full of distraction.

What does a spiritual practice include?

It may include making a commitment to stay in forgiveness, to live in gratitude and appreciation. It might mean regularly attending Sunday services, tithing, staying present to the Now moment and the next Now moment, seeing everything and everyone as a mirror of some aspect of you. Daily prayers and affirmations, setting intentions, visualization, visioning, mind treatments and more may be a part of it. It could simply be spending time in nature, fishing or taking a nice walk.

Your marriage or relationship with another can be a form of spiritual practice whereby one or both parties makes a commitment to bring their highest and best love and attention to their life together. A condition, a physical illness, or facing a problem could be your spiritual practice if you decide to look at it that way and make it one. Whatever fills your cup and gets you in touch with your joy is a personal way of taking care of yourself spiritually. What follows are some of my favorite practices, along with their explanations. These may help you get started on some of your own.

Affirmations

Affirmations are a great spiritual practice. One or two powerful lines that declare what you know to be true, or what you would like to believe as possible, can turn the way you think around in an instant. They are like a mantra. You say them throughout the day, or whenever you get caught up in the surrounding conditions or a negative mindset. They are instant pick-me-ups. They work quickly to change one's focus and shift thinking.

My first experience with affirmations was reading Catherine Ponder's, *Dynamic Laws of Prosperity*. I used her suggested affirmations to get me out of some very unpleasant conditions. One of my absolute favorites was something like, "You can't stand still without, if you are moving inside." I knew things were moving inside of me. My thinking was more positive than ever. Even though I couldn't see the changes on the outside happening yet, it was consoling to know and I trusted they would come. This practice supported me as I moved into a new philosophy and teaching, and my new life.

One of my classmates in my beginning Science of Mind classes, Jeff, became a good friend and running partner. At the time, we were studying "You Can Heal Your Life" by Louise Hay. Jeff was great at yelling out affirmations we had learned from the book as we ran through the streets of Midtown in Atlanta. I was a little timid about doing that at first. Soon it became second nature to me as well. I got to where I couldn't run without saying them. We even got our friend, Carol, to do them with us. I will always be grateful to Jeff for our precious time together, running and affirming. He was a great friend. He helped me break out of myself. I am also forever grateful to him for giving me an example of what a spiritual man looks like. He played a huge part in my demonstration of a life partner.

Forgiveness

Forgiveness is a practice that doesn't come easy. It takes some effort on our part to turn things around. It's always right to forgive. When asked how many times we should forgive, Jesus replied, "70 times 7". That's a lot of forgiveness. Pretty much, he was saying you can't forgive enough. Even if someone hasn't forgiven you, you need to forgive them. The most important reason to forgive is that it will set you free. It is vital for you to let go and move on. Whether you plan to see that person again or whether or not your paths ever cross in the future, it doesn't matter. It's the right thing for you to do.

I had a student who was very intelligent and had a big heart. She was going through some hard times which affected her studies and her plans to advance. I could only support her so far, though I really liked her a lot. She had some decisions to make. She decided to part company. I couldn't help ask what could I have done different? What was my part in what happened?

Four or five years later, we ran into each other. She confessed that what happened was perfect, and that it was never about what she *thought* it was about. She had learned a lot about herself. She thanked me for being her teacher and for all she learned from me. This was quite unexpected. I didn't need for it to happen. I had forgiven myself about it along the way. I welcomed it when it showed up. It was good to hear her process and the end result. The Universe is amazing. IT always works perfectly.

Most of all we need to forgive ourselves. Everyday there are things we wished we had done better, or had remembered to say or do. Forgiveness is for givingness to ourselves. It is essential to our health and well-being and always spiritually correct. It is a wonderful spiritual practice.

Giving Thanks

Gratitude and appreciation are another powerful, spiritual practice.

What are you thankful for today? Just asking the question helps us to look for the good. We are well trained to look and judge what is wrong, or what we don't like. We forget to focus in on all the good, and there is more good than not. It is easy to criticize and make a judgment. It takes effort to look at people and situations with love. When we do, we may be surprised to see all that is there.

Dr. Ernest Holmes, writes,

There is something in the universe which forever gives ITself to ITs creation, forever offers ITself, not as a sacrifice, but as an impartation of IT's essence into everything.

There is so much more going on than we are aware of in what happens all around us. If we were conscious of all the possible mis-takes, we would see just how precious and pivotal each moment really is. There is an Intelligence operating perfectly throughout the world. You and I wouldn't be here today or have gotten to this point in our lives if that were not true.

I love the story of Immaculee Ilibagiza, written in her book, *Left to Tell, Discovering God Amidst the Rwandan Holocaust.* She lives days on end hidden in a bathroom with a group of woman. There is no room to move. They are barely fed. Everyday they are spared a brutal death. She gets it that she is being saved for something special to do; otherwise, why would she exist in a time and a place where people all around her were being killed? What a revelation! This all came about because she stayed in the practice of prayer and meditation most of her waking hours. She was communing with the Infinite right where she was, cramped on the floor of a bathroom filled with others…receiving information she would otherwise not have known.

Ernest Holmes writes,

It is only as we come into union with good that we have the power of good. Evil blocks itself, congests its own efforts, dams its own streams, and destroys its own purpose. Good cannot be blocked.

So if good is freely given and cannot be blocked, what is getting in the way of us enjoying more of it? *We are.* What can we do then, to open ourselves up to our greater good?

One of the most important things we can do is to "Give Thanks". All the great spiritual masters recognized and taught the power of being grateful and the practice of giving thanks. Jesus was said to have said, "Father, I thank thee that thou hast heard me. And I know that thou hearest me always."

What more do we really need to say? It doesn't get any better than to see and experience God, Infinite Spirit, Life, continuously throughout our day, knowing that IT always hears us and immediately responds to us. Sometimes we don't see IT and yet, we forget that IT is the one giving us the ideas and so we need to prepare for the arrival of what it is we want. IT, The Thing ITself, God is always working. Giving thanks immediately puts us in right relationship with the Universe and opens us up to the greater flow of life and good. It is a prayer in and of itself.

Ho'oponopono

Ho'oponopono is an ancient, Hawaiian method of healing introduced recently by Joe Vitale in his book, *Zero Limits*. Dr. Hew Len has been working with this concept for years and healed an entire psychiatric wing while working in a state hospital in Hawaii. They were cured while he healed in his own mind how he was seeing them by continuously saying, "I love you, I am sorry. Please forgive me. Thank you." It is a powerful way of clearing and cleaning memories and unpleasant experiences with love and forgiveness of ourselves. Because we are responsible for everything we see and how we see it, and play a part in the creation of what is, it is up to us to see situations and people as their truth, as the pure, beautiful spirits that they are. This is a life changing experience that makes a huge difference for us all. It is a wonderful practice.

Ideal Day

Every morning write the essence of what you would like to experience for that day. You can probably do it the night before depending on your focus and energy at that time. You want to give this exercise your best time and energy because this will literally help you create the kind of day you want to experience; the kind of relationships you want to have; what kind of work you want to do; how much good you want to enjoy; how you want to experience yourself; and how you want to feel through it all. This is similar to setting your intention for what you would like to see happen, so you can zero in on your main focus for the day This is an expansion of that practice, an opportunity to get into the consciousness of your desire and do the behind the scenes work.

Emma Curtis Hopkins, a powerful teacher of the early 20th century said it this way, "Everyday, take time to sit and write. Name your good." Our thoughts are creative. It's like we are broadcasting a signal and that signal must manifest in physical form and experience. This is a great way to co-create with the Universe and live every day to the fullest. I have used this practice for years now and it continues to make a huge difference in my life. It helps me to remember that I am a powerful creator. When I stay in creation, I actively see my interplay with Life many times throughout the day. This daily work builds as I go and supports me in being all I can be, and in enjoying the creation of the huge garden of my life.

A full page copy of the Ideal Day Form can be found in the Addendum for an example or place to start.

Life As A Mirror

Seeing everything and everyone in your life as a mirror of who *you* are is a form of spiritual practice. Looking at everyone and everything as a reflection of ourselves helps us to see those aspects of ourselves we may not be aware of. We can only see in others what is also in us. Some aspects may be pleasing and some may not depending on what they are. They may even be disturbing. How could I ever be like that you might wonder?

A long time ago, there was a person in my life that really aggravated me. The situation we were in would have been awkward for anyone in our shoes. I couldn't figure out what to do about how I felt about her. It seemed like we were complete opposites. The irritation, the disturbance intensified every time I thought of her, and whenever our paths crossed, which happened often. It seemed as though I would never break free of feeling this way. The rest of my life was going so well. I didn't need this, nor did I understand why she made me feel this way.

I knew it was true that we attract what we are, so I started treating my mind about it. I knew this all had to be more about me than it was about her because I didn't even really know her. I needed this bad feeling to end. Then one day I saw that aspect of distaste I felt about her in myself. That put me in my place and took care of it immediately. Anytime, the bad feeling came back, I just had to remind myself of that part of me and love myself. I knew what work I needed to do. Once I saw that I could be like her, and that I was just projecting, it stopped. She ceased to offend me and I was able to look at her with love. Even more I was able to love that part of myself and heal it.

Meditation

Meditation is another form of spiritual practice. It's a process of stilling the mind and body; allowing one's self to listen. The Universe is speaking all the time. How many of us know how to listen and hear what's being said? Some people believe they have to keep a conversation going continuously with anyone who will listen. No dead space for them. Others can't live without the TV, music on, or some kind of noise, at all times. It is a whole new experience to feel comfortable enough with your self to be quiet and function in silence.

For years it was difficult for me to sit still long enough to meditate. I always enjoyed "Walking Meditation" because it keeps my body active and allows my mind to *be* and enjoy. I receive much clarity in that state. My walks are for the purpose of being in nature, soaking in all its energy and listening. It is there that I am able to hear myself think and hear beyond the self talk of my mind.

In recent years, it has become much easier to sit and be still. Great good is derived from spending time that way which may not be obvious to the casual observer or to the beginner. In time, you begin to notice the subtle, quiet shifts, perceptions and benefits. Soon you realize you want more and can't imagine life without your meditative time.

Power of Intention

Wayne Dyer wrote a wonderful book called, *The Power of Intention*". Intention, or intending, is a powerful, spiritual practice. Before you start your day, ask yourself, "What is my intention for this day, this phone call, this meeting?" John and I ask our son, Joseph, every morning, "What kind of day are you going to have?" We have been doing it since he was quite young. Most of the time, he says, "A fun day". Depending on what is going on, whether he needs extra help in a certain area, he may include something more specific like "Enjoy good friends".

Asking yourself, "What is my intention?" gives you time to think about what you want to accomplish and how you want to *be*. How do you want to feel during the process and especially feel as an end result? Instead of assuming that things are going to go well on their own, or leaving things up to the law of averages which means you win some, lose some, you put yourself in the driver's seat and co-create with the Infinite the best possible outcome for all involved. Experiences are sure to go well if you are prepared. "Hard to have" conversations are easier if your intentions are genuine and loving. If you come from an open, loving place, your results will be better and you won't have to look back wishing things could have been different.

Setting your intention is getting as much consciousness as possible behind your encounter so that you may enjoy a richer, fuller experience of it. Doing this puts you in a co-creative role with the Universe instead of a reactionary one. When you set your intention, the Universe gets to work and shows up in the most interesting ways.

Example:

My intention for this week is for Spirit to have some fun through me, and all those around me. I want to enjoy this time and know I am supported. I want to lighten up and know that Spirit makes a very special and meaningful meeting for us all. My work load is light. I play my part and know the right and perfect people step up to play the rest of the parts and we all work together as one in perfect synchronicity. Love abounds. It is truly a celebration of Life and all that is good. Thank you God! And so it is!

Sacred Covenant

A sacred covenant is a finely tuned agreement that you create between yourself and the Infinite, updated and changed along the way as you gain greater clarity. This is what you live by. These are the rules of your life. They help you stay on track. Charles and Myrtle Fillmore, founders of Unity, created a beautiful covenant with God. In exchange for being taken care of and supported by the Infinite, they agreed to dedicate their lives to their work and to helping people live greatly. Very Powerful!

The covenant also clarifies what is yours to do and what is God's. It can bring you great peace of mind about life. Once you get it down, and know it well, you carry it with you in your heart and it is always available to draw upon whenever you need or want. It is a beautiful spiritual practice.

Here are some suggested steps…

The following is my Sacred Covenant:

I Am Here To:

I am here to experience more God; to experience myself as god; to support others in experiencing more God, experiencing themselves as god and in supporting others to do the same.

I AM:

I am a clear, practical teacher of the Truth. I am a powerful voice for God.

I Agree To:

I agree to be the fullest expression of Spirit I came here to be; to come from the highest, most loving, abundant consciousness at all times; to love, respect, and value myself, my life and my work, and love, respect, and value others, their lives, and their work; to see the perfection of God in everyone and everything, especially in myself and my family; to bring my best love and attention to everyone and everything this day and every day.

The Universe Agrees To:

The Universe agrees to love and support us; to orchestrate our lives; to divinely place me and my family in the right and perfect situations where we experience the greatest ease, prosperity and joy.

I Am Grateful For:

I am grateful for our ever deepening, expanding partnership together.

I Dedicate My Life To:

I dedicate my life to the one Life we are all living together.

The Universe Dedicates IT's Life To:

The Universe dedicates IT's Life to helping us realize that we are already free.

And So It Is!

* A full page copy can be found in the Addendum

Sacred Space Covenant

If we believe that Good or God is infinite, which means IT is everywhere, then every place is sacred space, not just a church or a shrine, but everywhere all at the same time. Sometimes it is helpful to recognize and remember just how special it is right where we are. It's hard to believe that all of God is present at every point of existence which means right where I am and right where you are. No matter how dark or dreary the place, physically or mentally, it is empowering to remember we are standing on sacred ground and always immersed in Spirit.

By consciously focusing on the Presence and Power that we live in and are immersed in, we can create special places that support the harmony and balance we need in our homes, in our workplace, and everywhere we come together with others. We can accomplish great things when we have first created a safe, sacred place where we can be ourselves and express openly.

The idea of a Sacred Space Covenant came about years ago when a student in class said she did not feel safe to speak and share. It was an upper level class which included some strong personalities who were convinced they knew all the answers. It was a challenge for us all. A way to get the whole class to respect others' perspectives and stay on the same page, was to create the following covenant, which made all the difference.

Sacred Space Covenant

I live in a universe that welcomes me just as I am. IT, God, created me as a perfect expression of ITself. IT accepts me with unconditional love and provides me with the space I need to live comfortably and easily. I know this sacred space is essential to my well being. It frees me to accept my humanness, my imperfections and more and more appreciate my divine nature.

I freely and lovingly make this kind of space available to others who are near me, allowing them to be their real and true selves. I extend my heart, I provide the wisdom available to me when asked, and choose words which neither impose nor judge but guide others in knowing what is right for them. I am divinely supported in knowing how to do this.

I give thanks for knowing sacred space is provided for us all. I enjoy living in a universe of love. And so it is!

I agree to listen and be present, and not try to fix or give advice.

I agree to bring my best love and attention to whatever or whomever is before me, including, and especially, myself.

I agree to practice non-judgment.

I agree to love and accept myself and others as they are.

I agree to stay in the present, the *now* moment of Power.

I use as my guide:

"If it is loving, if it grows, expands or deepens love, it's the right thing to do!"

Signed _____ Dated_____

Spiritual Autobiography

I like what my brother, Tom, said recently during a visit to Orlando. "You don't even know me. Maybe you have spent a handful of days with me over the past 5 years." It's true. Coming from a large family and living long distance from one another, there is very little quality, one on one time available to get to know one another.

If this is true about the relationships we have with others, how well do we really know ourselves? How much time do we take with ourselves reflecting, contemplating and appreciating who we are and what we have created in our lives? Getting to know ourselves amidst a busy life is essential to taking care of ourselves. Take time to review what you have done in the past. Take a look at what you have been involved in throughout your life. Have the courage to look closely at your "stuff".

Here are some questions you might consider:

Who were the key players in your life?

Who were the people who influenced your thinking and values?

What events, circumstances and situations happened that helped make you who you are today?

Who were your spiritual teachers, writers that touched you and helped you open up? Strangers that said something you will never forget?

How has your concept of God changed through the years? What was your first idea of God, what has it evolved to over the years, and what is it now? Where would you like it to be?

What shifts took place in your thinking that turned things around for you? What gifts came out of the difficult years?

What did you do that really made you happy?

What brought you to the point where you are now on your spiritual path?

When we take a look at what has been, we will see things we weren't able to notice before and appreciate how perfectly the divine hand of Life was at work all along. Our spiritual autobiography gives us a long range perspective, more of the real story. We can appreciate our very own spiritual awakening and see how perfectly things unfolded to support us in being all we came here to be. It's easy to forget how much love and support there really was along the way even if it was only a vague sense of belonging to Life.

You will be amazed at what you find when you really look. This is a great exercise to help you appreciate all the gifts you have been given along the way. You may be surprised at how many of them there really are. Even though there are things you might like to forget, you may be able to see them in a new light from where you stand now. This helps set the stage for future work. It's a great place to start. When we see intelligence has been at work all along, it will help us to trust that we are always in divine hands and that our future will proceed with the same guarantee. Going through this process can help us reevaluate our past and appreciate more of it.

Staying Present

Staying in the *now* moment is a great spiritual practice. One of the biggest gifts I ever received was the message so clearly given by Eckert Tolle in his book, *Power of Now*. What a revelation! I had been studying for quite awhile, and this was not a new idea. The way he presented his message hit me between the eyes. I could finally say "I got it!" with my entire being. The *now* moment is a portal to the divine. This is where the stuff of Life happens. When we take our power back from past experiences, such as what went wrong, or future ones, what is going to happen, and focus on enjoying this precious moment we are in, it frees us. It frees us to live fully the richness of each moment and be open to so much more than we ever thought possible. It takes us deeper into the great wealth that is going on within and around us versus just surface or superficial living. This practice continuously opens us up to more of what we need to know in order to live our lives from a higher, more expanded consciousness.

Tithing or Regular Committed Giving

Everyone wants to give. Everyone wants to participate in a bigger idea than just themselves or their lives even if they don't know it yet. I was a committed giver before I ever tried tithing. I started giving what I thought I could. One day, my cousin, Walter, saw what I was giving and said, "You can do better". He was right. I could and I did. Every time I increased it from there, the flow came back to me increased.

Then one day I graduated to tithing and I have never gone back. Tithing is a great tool to stretch us in our giving and help us know how much we are capable of giving. I had no idea that I could give so much. Typically, tithing means 10% of what you bring in. Tithing is like training wheels. You keep them on as long as you need them and then you go beyond them. One tither said, "I want to make so much money, that I live on 10% and give the rest away." That's a big idea. I have found that the more I stretch in what I am giving, the more prosperity I enjoy, the bigger I feel, the more I realize how much I am making a contribution to my world. It helps me show my appreciation for all that has been given to me and my family. It gives me a sense of ownership of the world.

Knowing I am one with Life brings me great joy which keeps me in the flow.

Visioning

Visioning is a spiritual practice created by Dr. Michael Beckwith, founder of the Agape International Spiritual Center in Los Angeles. This process is used when you don't know what you want, or when you have decided that your life, or a certain experience, no longer has to be limited to what you decide it can be. The ego, as wonderful and necessary as it is, insists on having things its way. In this practice, you recognize yourself as a spiritual being who has made a decision to be open to what Spirit or the Universe wants to do through you. You ask questions and then listen from a deeper place within where you are in touch with a greater, more expansive awareness. It's getting into the consciousness of what you are feeling and desiring as much as possible and releasing how you think things need to look or play out. You stay open and receptive to new ideas you never thought of before.

Some of the other questions you ask are: what gifts or talents do I bring to this experience; what must I embrace in order for this to happen; what must I release and what do I need to know now.

You may or may not get instant results. Sometimes inspirations and solutions come later in unexpected moments. As you practice, you will learn to appreciate the subtle and sometimes surprising ways ideas come and change happens. This is another great practice.

Visualization

Visualizing is: Picturing how you want things to be. Using your imagination and stretching your mind to think about what is possible. Taking time to fantasize, daydream or pretend what your life could be, seeing what some area of your life might look like in your mind's eye. Seeing your dreams come true there. Seeing yourself living in the newly conceived picture and spending time there in your mind regularly until the picture unfolds in your outer world. This is a great spiritual practice, especially if you know what you want. If you don't know what you want, this practice will take you closer to what that might be. It stretches your imagination muscles.

12
Mind Treatment

Spiritual Evolution should make the Infinite not more distant, but more intimate.

Ernest Holmes
Science of Mind

When the mind loses its density, you become translucent, like the flower. Spirit – the formless – shines through you into this world.

Eckert Tolle
Power of Now

The movie, "A Beautiful Mind", was based on the life of John Forbes Nash, Jr., a Nobel Laureate in Economics. At the end of the movie, Russell Crow, the actor, playing the part of John, who has the mind of a genius that had gone over the edge, is walking out of a building. His mind fragments. He sees the two figures standing on the side watching him, trying to grab his attention as he walks out of the building having a conversation with others. These two are the main characters in his head, the voices he hears. He can't help but notice them, there, because they have been with him for a very long time even though, now, he is in a much healthier place. They remain. What's different now from what he experienced in the past? In the past, he would have engaged them. Now he chooses to ignore them and keeps walking.

We all have some version of those destructive voices (devils of our own making). If we continue to listen to them, they will take us down. He rises above them, not by pretending they don't exist, and not by giving them their say. He triumphs because he understands that he is not his mind, but the thinker behind the mind. The thinker behind the mind is in the driver's seat and can choose what thoughts to think or not to think.

Each one of us has the same choice to make at any given time. We have the opportunity to make the right choices for ourselves that will make all the difference. Even when that isn't so easy and we continue to hear the other voice, the voice of fear, the voice of doubt, or the voice that says we aren't good enough, we can choose again.

When I think of what my mind is like now compared to what it once was, I am amazed at the progression and how far I have come. I know it will only continue to evolve. It's typically not something you think about. An undeveloped mind can easily be distracted. A disturbed mind can play an upsetting scene over and over again for weeks, replaying it as if it had just happened. We sometimes relive the emotions until we are so sick and tired we finally let it go of them because we are worn out.

I had a student whom I worked with years ago that I couldn't understand the material we were studying. Granted some of that could have been my inexperience teaching this subject matter at the time. He would respond to a question and his answer didn't make sense. It was as if he were speaking Greek to me. He thought he was clear. He eventually did get clear as he worked on himself. That's where Mind Treatment comes in: it reorganizes our thought processes.

When I first started attending a New Thought, Science of Mind Center and classes, I began to feel better just by hearing healthy, more loving ideas, new ways of looking at Life. Being together with others who were thinking the same way, serious about working on themselves and wanting to create a better life, encouraged me to do the same. For the first time, in a really long time, I was happy. I had improved so much in the first two years I didn't even know that there was something more I could do to have greater control over the direction of my life. I remember asking, "You mean there is more?"

Absolutely there is always more. I didn't know I was about to learn how to use a mental tool that I would depend on daily for the rest of my life, sometimes three or four or more times a day to shift my consciousness, my perspective, my thinking, on the spot. In order to know what I really needed to know from a place of Universal Truth, and know the highest possible thoughts about myself, others, and any and all situations. This was the practice for me.

I had experienced Mind Treatments on Sundays, and in class done in a group. I even went to see a Practitioner to receive my first private treatment. I am forever grateful for that, otherwise I might still be living alone. I wanted to have a loving partner. Rev. Karen Wolfson helped me with this. Thanks to Karen and treatment I share my life with a wonderful man.

One day a light bulb went on, and it dawned on me that I could learn how to do this for myself. It was time to learn the process. Once I started learning how to do that for myself, it was watch out world! My good friend, Carol, and I would spend hours and hours discussing and writing treatments about what we wanted to create and experience in our new lives. We were creating, consciously, for the first time in our lives. It was a very exciting time for us and actually still is. It really hasn't stopped.

Not long after we started, John came into my life and she said, I want a guy just like him. Soon after, she demonstrated her own version of John for herself, a nice guy, who dearly loves her and is a dedicated family man. We had a good laugh, and still do, at how much he even looks like John.

What is Mind Treatment?

Is it something done to you? What does it entail? Is it possible for anyone and can they do it for themselves? What about doing it for others? What's it all about?

These days we get all kinds of treatments: massages, pedicures, reflexology, facials, and skin treatments. There are all kinds of things to do for ourselves. Mind Treatment is no different. It can be done for you, and/or it can be done by you for yourself and for others.

What does it do?

The practice of it helps us to:

Center our minds

Sit in the director's seat

Clarify our thought processes

Focus on healthier ways of looking at things

Shifts consciousness to change our awareness

Broadens our perspectives

When most people have a thought they think this thought, or belief is theirs for keeps. They possess it. It becomes a part of them. They hang onto it and are attached to it. Just because they have a particular thought, they believe it must be right for them. It is who they are. They are afraid to have their ideas challenged in any way because they believe they are

173

their thoughts. What they don't know is that they are not their thoughts. They are something more than any thought they may ever have.

People hang on to their thoughts because they don't realize that there are many other wonderful ideas where that thought came from. There is an Infinite Mind to draw upon which is endless and infinite in IT's Intelligence, and that we can be in touch with possibilities and explanations that go beyond our smaller minds. There is not a problem this Intelligence can't handle. As we get in touch with how Life really works, we will find there are always clearer and better ways to think.

Mind Treatment is really a form of prayer. Often times, it is called affirmative prayer because it is made up of definite, positive statements of Truth. It is not begging, bargaining or beseeching with a distant deity who needs convincing and only comes around every now and then. Rather, it is recognizing that God is all there is.

There is no other Power in the Universe.

We are one with the Creator.

We are expressions of IT.

IT is here to support us.

IT wants us to succeed.

IT provides for us as it does for all IT's creations.

This is a tool to shift consciousness out of the obvious condition into the spiritual realm of Truth. It's called treatment because it treats our minds. It gets our minds into alignment with Universal Mind, or Spirit.

This is an active, alive, conscious communication with the Beloved. It's not talking to some entity separate from ourselves. It goes beyond prayer as we know it. It is not a passive thing like meditation. Meditation is more of a quieting and listening. Some call it a prayer treatment to signify that it is still very much a prayer – a more evolved form of prayer, one that engages us in an active, ongoing participation with Life. As we relate intellectually to the Infinite Intelligence of the Universe, we experience extraordinary results. Life becomes much more exciting, and we quickly see the game of Life is the only real game in town.

I use seven steps to a full Mind Treatment. You can use all seven, or fewer. It's helpful to be familiar with them all, as different circumstances require a greater shift to be made in consciousness.

Step 1) I recognize a higher power.

Step 2) I remind myself that I am *one* with IT.

Step 3) I embody the idea I am creating of (health, wholeness, perfection, abundance, whatever it is.)

Step 4) I see what happens to be in my way and release it. I recognize a fear or a doubt or a sense of giving my power away in a situation and I release it. "I release my doubts about this happening now. I just let them go." Just like in "A Beautiful Mind" I see them and I keep on going.

Step 5) More strongly than ever, I affirm what I know to be my real truth about the situation.

Step 6) I give thanks.

Step 7) I am complete. I release it. "And so it is!"

Spiritual Mind Treatment is a proven tool for shifting consciousness. It was originally designed by Ernest Holmes, founder of Science of Mind after all of his studies of world religions, teachings, philosophies and personal experiences. It is most often taught as a five step method.

example

Mind Treatment

Focus: Feeling Joy

Step 1: Recognition

I believe in a Universe that is perfect. Everything IT creates is done in a loving, creative and joyful way.

Step 2: Unification

I am *one* with the Universe. I was created in love and joy.

Step 3: Affirmation

Therefore, love and joy are at the very heart of me. The very core of my being is joy. I experience love and joy now and always.

Step 4: Denial*

Nothing or no one can get in the way of my joy, not even me.

Step 5: Reaffirmation*

I am joy itself. I enjoy this day, my life and my world always.

Step 6: Gratitude

I am grateful in advance for the magnificent opportunity to joyfully express the freedom of Spirit that I AM.

Step 7: Release

And so it is!

*Optional steps

**See the addendum for a form to create your own

You Just Have to Know

There's a lot of talk these days about vibrating at a higher energy in order to more easily manifest our good. We are made of energy so we need to be in tune, or vibrationally aligned with what we say we want to see first. When we understand that we create our experience, then we want to make sure we are creating more of what we want and less of what we don't want. We can't necessarily maintain a high energy level about an idea we would like to see 24/7. We can *know* in our minds, and believe in our hearts that whatever we desire is already ours until we see it come into physical form. Believing is seeing versus seeing is believing. Being a law, our desire must come into being. There is no holding thoughts or even sending them. All we have to do is *know*.

Once one has an idea, it is known in Universal Mind immediately. Anyone of us who is receptive to that particular information has access to it. We are all tapped into this Mind whether we realize it or not. The Universe takes care of the rest. If you *know* that you already have what you want to demonstrate in your mind, then it is already done in the Mind of God or Universal Mind. You are already vibrating on a higher plane and will naturally and easily manifest your heart's desires and those things you need to live a creative, wonderful life. You will experience yourself in greater and more expansive ways.

We can't possibly be excited all the time and keep an idea alive that way. We couldn't generate enough enthusiasm and excitement to last. Some ideas take longer to manifest than others. But we can always *know*. When you *know*, you know it's already done. It's a done deal. It just has to play out in the physical realm. This puts us in a co-creative position with the Infinite. Empowering, isn't it?

In 1909, Thomas Troward wrote in his *Edinburgh Lectures on Mental Science*,

Because he is what he is and leads the van of the evolutionary procession, if man is to evolve further, it can now only be by his own conscious cooperation with the law which has brought him to the standpoint where he is able to realize that such a law exists.

No Better Investment

You are the one who will never leave you. That is just the way it is. It doesn't mean you aren't loved. It means you are the one who loves you the most. Not because anyone else isn't trying. The others in your life love you the best they can. Everyone has to take care of themselves while we are here. That is our responsibility, and not someone else's. No one else can do this for you. You must do this for yourself. The man or woman of your dreams will not, and cannot do this for you. No one else can make you happy. The quicker you see this, the quicker you understand that all the Spirit, all the Power and Presence of God is right where you are for you to use. Everything you could ever need or want in the way of substance is right here waiting for you to call IT forth and make more good out of IT. I can't think of any better investment than learning how to use your mind. I can't think of any better way to spend your time, energy and money than learning and refining your thought process to include life-supporting ideas such as these. Your consciousness is what lives on when you go.

There is always more to learn, always more of ourselves to experience. There's more of God, the Tao, Spirit, whatever you call this immense presence that we live in, to understand and appreciate. How much more can I utilize the rest of my days knowing what I know? You can have all that, too, and give back to the world in even more satisfying and fulfilling ways for the greater good of all.

Our spiritual practices are an investment into ourselves. They build a greater capacity within us, and then we tend to go to God when there is a problem. The most difficult time to try to find peace is when you are down and out. At times like that it feels like we're climbing out of sludge on the riverbank. While most of us have found God in the middle of our worst situations, the best time to pray is when things are going well. When you are so filled up with Life you are the most powerful, so it is the strongest time to do mind treatment and enjoy the best Life has to offer.

A good mind is a terrible thing to waste.

Thank you God for a beautiful Mind! It's a true gift. I cherish mine and vow to use it wisely. I invite you to do the same.

"I Have Control Over My Mind and So Do YOU!"

13
Building Your Spiritual Portfolio (More tools)

Such is the power of right thinking that it cancels and erases everything unlike itself. It answers every question, solves all problems, is the solution to every difficulty. It is like the Sunlight of Eternal Truth bursting through the clouds of obscurity and bathing all like in a celestial glory. It is the Absolute with which we are dealing and nothing less.

Ernest Holmes
Science of Mind

What do you really want out of life?

What have you been denying yourself that you would really enjoy?

Are you willing to invest in yourself and do the necessary work to get what you want? In other words are you ready to work on yourself? That's what it's going to take.

This is so natural for children. Watch them. They are our greatest teachers. They know how to do this, and there was a time when we knew too. Somewhere along the way, we forgot. They know only possibility. We got off track when the adults in our lives, who were asleep to their divine nature, told us we couldn't do something. It doesn't matter how well meaning they were it didn't serve us.

Continuously hearing we "can't do this, or can't do that", beat us into submission and we find ourselves living in a world that is immersed in the appearance of lack and limitation. We think we are in touch with reality. We give too much attention to reacting to what is happening and thinking that is the only reality. We are intellectually smart and yet, what do we really know? The proof is always in the pudding. What is the quality of our life and experience?

Listen to your heart. Say yes to your dreams and desires. Live in gratitude, and appreciation. Have a great attitude about all things in your life. Look at them closely. Look at the people and the joy they bring you; the things you have going in your life; how far you have come; who you are today; what is true about you spiritually. You are perfect in the eyes of God, always have been and always will be. Putting our attention on thanksgiving prepares your mind to see how much abundance you already have and focuses you in a way that allows you to receive more.

It may be difficult to be thankful when things do not go as planned. A cousin or aunt shows up at your doorstep, needing help, wanting to visit, maybe even wanting to move in…whatever it is that takes us by surprise. Is it possible for us to go along with the change of plans and see that there is a gift? Remember "The Guest House" by Rumi?

THE GUEST HOUSE
This Being Human is a Guest House.
Every Morning a New Arrival.
A Joy, a Depression, A Meanness,
Some Momentary Awareness comes
As an unexpected Visitor.

Welcome and Entertain them All!
Even if they're a Crowd of Sorrows,
Who violently sweep your House
Empty of It's Furniture,
Still, treat each Guest honorably.
He may be clearing You out
For some new Delight!

The Dark Thought, the Shame, the Malice,
Meet them all at the Door laughing,
And invite Them in.

Be grateful for Whoever comes
Because each Guest has been sent
As a Guide from beyond.

Rumi

Can we playfully go along with the surprise guests or happenings and just say "Yes" instead of reacting, getting upset or having it go the way we think it should? Maybe can we whisper to ourselves, "Spirit this is very interesting. What do you have in mind for me or us, here? I know

ce so this must be perfect. What is the gift in
ft in this for us? What do I need to know here?
te?"

ing there for us. Once the awareness arises and
answer appears and once again you see the
T's thing in your life.

The banquet table has been set. We get to
if that's all you think you can ask for, or you
ocolate cake. You can stay home and passively
out their roles, or you can invite friends over,
pecial place and spend quality time together,
ch they mean to you; spend quality time with
preparation for getting some new ideas to set
active participant in life!

It's your choice and you always have the option. It's all about creative ways to express that which we hold dear to our hearts. It's all about having fun, spreading love, growing love right where we are, with whatever we have to work with.

Let the child in you come out and play. Turn on that light inside and see it shine more brightly than ever. Feel the connection we have to one another. Feel the joy. Be happy. Things don't have to look like you think they have to look. Invite Spirit into your life in a new way and watch all the different ways IT shows up. Let the good times roll.

Material things are good, too. It's all God. It's all energy. We were meant to enjoy nice things. They are the icing on the cake, the extras. "Seek first the kingdom and all things will be added". Once you have the main recipe in place, you can enjoy them. You have permission to spend money on yourself. Some of you already know how to do that, and may do it too well. For others, it is a big deal.

I watched my son, who was eight at the time, shop at the school's holiday store. The first day, he came home with presents for himself. I started to say something to him about Christmas being a time to buy for others, and letting them buy for you (blah, blah, blah). I stopped myself because he was right. Why not buy for yourself? It took me way too long to figure out I could buy myself presents, and give up waiting for someone else to get the hint about what I wanted.

After my divorce, it felt strange not to wear my wedding ring. I already felt strange enough, that was just more obvious because I always loved a nice ring. My fingers felt naked. I had a boyfriend but we had no plans to move forward with our relationship. There was no ring possibility in sight.

One day, it dawned on me that I could buy myself a nice ring. What a concept! I picked out a small gold rose with a diamond chip in the middle. It was perfect. It was close to Mother's Day which was an especially difficult day for me because my kids and I were miles apart. I decided that I would celebrate myself as a Mother with that special ring. After all, I *was* still a Mother and I was doing everything I knew to stay close to my children and love and support them from afar. It felt so good to be able to do that for myself.

I was in my early 30's before I got the idea that I could do something special for myself. Joseph, my son, just saved himself years and years of waiting and disappointment by buying for himself. God is all there is. Sometimes something new will help shift us into a new paradigm or experience and open us up in new ways. Everything and everyone works together for Good. That is the way of Life…perfect and so are you and so am I. And so it is!

"I Have Everything I Need. I Am Well Supported and So Are YOU!"

Part 4
Where Do We Go From Here?

14
It's All Here

Recently, I spent time in my little refuge, a wonderful wildlife center in the middle of suburbia, Lake Lotus Park, and found I had the park to myself except for the park rangers who have become friends through the years.

I had heard there were lots of gators, otters, owls and about four or five bobcats in the park at the time. I just hadn't seen them yet. I asked one of the rangers what were my chances of seeing a bobcat? He said they were good. So I was looked very closely and walked quietly. I didn't want to miss a thing.

This went on for awhile and nothing happened. I wasn't seeing anything. Then I realized that my serious search and extra effort made me miss seeing this wildlife. I had expectations, and I was setting myself up for disappointment. I was restless. This was not good.

So, I stopped all that and decided instead to enjoy myself. It felt right to let go of my agenda, absorb the energy and beauty of the surroundings. I got into "the zone". It was great to just receive and I said to myself, "If there is something I would very much like to see, Intelligence will point it out to me. IT will get my attention." That was so freeing. It felt so good to relax and be.

Shortly after that, something did get my attention. I heard movement in the water by the shore where I was walking. There was small opening in the brush at the water's edge and as I looked down from the boardwalk, up popped this otter head and then next to it, another. Two cute, little otters were staring up at me, and then proceeded to go back into the water. I was elated.

Looking back at the incident, it seems almost as if it didn't really happen. For me it has never happened quite like that again. I have had other wonderful, wildlife adventures but not that exact one. The Universe never repeats ITself or does the same things twice. Why would IT when IT has infinite options. IT continuously creates anew.

If you google animal totems, otters remind us that everything is interesting if we look at it from the right angle. They represent the feminine side, joy. If an otter has entered your life, it may be time to find some play in your life, to awaken your inner child.

Seeing those otters definitely awakened my inner child, and the experience reminded me of how we must live if we are to enjoy life the way it was meant to be enjoyed. It reminded me that when we are appreciating all the life and beauty around us, we are open. That's "Being". That's the "I AM" presence as us, our greater self, our spirit. When we are the "I AM" presence as us, we can be open to what Life wants to share with us at that moment. Searching says we don't have what we want and so we continue to not see or have. Beingness says it's already here. It is time to *be*.

The whole experience of living is really something more than what appears on the surface. There is more here for us to examine and more to know about ourselves.

"It's All Here For Me. It's Been Here All Along and It's Here For YOU Too!"

15
Love Yourself Anyway

Love is the grandest healing and drawing power on earth. It is the very reason for our being, and that explains why it is that people should have something or someone to love. The life that has not loved has not lived, it is still dead.

Ernest Holmes
Science of Mind

Sometimes we get very lost. Along the way, there have been times when I have gotten way off track. Recently, during the writing of this book, as I mentioned earlier, my mother made her transition or passed on. While it was an amazing experience to go through with her, months after, I felt myself drifting. I wasn't quite over it yet. I want to be. I try to be. It just isn't happening.

This became clear to me when I came down with a knock-you-out flu that was going around. I don't usually get those things. Days later as I attempted to gain some kind of normalcy and build myself up, I decided to take a walk. I took one of my regular routes down a parkway close to home. Along the way I stopped at the clubhouse and the gazebo overlooking the lake. Later as I continued on, I ran across an elderly man who had stopped to see a magnificent, red shouldered hawk, which we both admired. It felt good to get some exercise and clear my head on such a beautiful day. An hour or so later, when I got home, I discovered that somewhere along the way, I had lost my keys.

My husband and son were running errands. The doors were locked. I didn't have a cell phone with me. I was able to get into the back porch where I sat wondered what to do. I asked myself, "Do I wait, or do I go back and see if my keys are somewhere along the way?" Too restless to wait, meditate and do nothing, I decided to retrace my steps. I wasn't sure I had the energy to go another two and a half miles. I didn't have water which is important in the Florida heat. I had eaten a big breakfast and that was a good thing.

I was not as excited as I was the first time I made that walk. In fact, I was wishing I was Samantha, the witch, and could just wiggle my nose and be there. I rarely lose things, and I was a bit disturbed. I have never lost the keys to my car and my house at the same time. Not a good sign metaphysically. You have to have keys. I really was living in a cloud.

I continued to make the journey, step by step. I checked the clubhouse, even asked the attendant. No sign of them. I headed to the gazebo. They were less likely to be there. Tired and frustrated because there were others things that needed to get done, I surrendered to my process. I came close to crying. I had made the best of it so far and now my strength was waning. Then something inside of me said, "Don't cry" and inferred that crying was an inappropriate response to be having in the midst of this extraordinary day with Mother Nature. I have always loved the great outdoors. I rarely get as much time out there as I would like and today, was the perfect opportunity to stay out in it. In fact, when I really thought about it, I had been secretly craving more time outside.

How often do we get frustrated on our path and want to turn in the towel when what is happening is for our benefit? It might very well be something we have asked for. So, with that realization, I said to myself there must be a good reason for me to be out here even if I don't know what it is yet. Maybe the universe has something special to show me. As I approached the gazebo, I heard loud bird noises. A flock of mourning doves had clearly been disturbed and flew away. Who disturbed them? I walked slowly, looking carefully through the branches and leaves. And then, I saw him. He was a gorgeous, pileated woodpecker, a huge bird with dark black feathered body and white markings and a bright red tuft of hair on his head. You can't help but smile when you see such a creature of beauty and stature.

I was able to tip toe quietly past him without running him off. I was in the gazebo now. No keys in sight. Now, it no longer mattered. Who needs keys? The gift of seeing one of these birds made it all worthwhile.

To add to my delight, I saw another something red flash in a tree right next to the boardwalk. It was his mate. They were a pair and they were so beautiful. I could have stayed for hours watching them. With great dignity and style, they positioned themselves, studying the tree, and then pecked away for the gems hiding beneath the surface.

What a gift! Life's message to me that day was to slow down and enjoy the scenery. When we get weary and the road seems like the one we traveled before, we need to remember there is some gem waiting to be discovered. Nothing is without purpose. Can it really be that everything is here for my delight? That I just have to get below the surface of what I am feeling to the truth of what is really there? God is good. Spirit is all there is. How can there be anything else but good?

It occurred to me that I was still recovering from the loss of my mother. Maybe I am exactly where I am supposed to be. Where I am is where I need to be and that's okay. Wherever you are is perfectly okay as well. When you are ready for more, you will know. Giving ourselves permission to just *be* is loving ourselves and gives permission to those around us to do what they need to do for themselves, too. How freeing is that?

"I Fully Love And Accept Myself No Matter What, and So Can YOU!"

16
Smooth Sailing

You cannot stay on the summit forever;
You have to come down again…
So why bother in the first place?
Just this: What is above knows what is below,
But what is below does not know what is above.

One climbs, one sees.
One descends, one sees no longer,
But one has seen.

There is an art of conducting oneself
In the lower regions
By the memory of what one saw higher up.

When one can no longer see,
One can at least still know.

Attributed to Rene Daumal
from Mount Analogue, found in *Compass Points* by Frank Henninger

No one can take what you know, your knowing, away from you. There are things that can only be known to us if we climb to higher ground, and while we must come down the mountain again, we will never forget those things we saw and we will never be the same because of it. We will be a much better person because of what we have seen and felt and now know.

Seven years ago, when a close friend of mine in Atlanta discovered she had breast cancer, we communicated mainly by phone, which is not so easy during difficult times. I also know it was perfect in its own way because I was not caught up in the changes that she went through, like losing hair etc. from chemo. Even more, I did not have to watch one of the most beautiful women I know, suffer. I could stay focused on knowing that cancer was not her truth, that she was more than she appeared to be, and that she could rise above this. That was my advantage. I could maintain my perfect picture of her mentally.

My disadvantage was connecting with her on the emotional level as my friend. It was hard for me to insist on her truth and be there for her, too, with her process.

One day while on vacation I ran across an attractive, woman's sports top with a sailboat embroidered on it and underneath were the words, "Smooth Sailing". I immediately thought of Carol. It was so perfect. I bought it and sent it to her. The words were comforting to her and she held onto them with the visual of the sailboat.

Now, years later, it was my turn to face something very difficult. My own mother had been dying for the past few years and things were coming to a point where it really was becoming a reality. One day while talking about it to Carol, she said, "Remember". I replied, "Remember what?" She said, "Smooth Sailing". I breathed a sigh of relief. Of course, "Smooth Sailing" applied here as well. I framed the most beautiful picture of my mother I could find and placed it on my desk with a sticky note saying, "Smooth Sailing". This helped me keep in mind my intention for her transition and the process we were all going through with her.

As we come to the close of this book, I leave these words with you as well: "Smooth Sailing" to you. I know there are places and times, situations and circumstances, where just recalling those words will bring you comfort and help you remember that it can be smooth, whatever the storm. There are experiences that we must face seemingly alone. There is a Presence and Power available to us to use. We are never alone even when we think we are.

Anytime we don't like what is going on, we can change it. We don't have to spend years and years bogged down with processing our negative emotions, or indulging a belief that we have to carry our past and hang on to our "story". We can put an end to all of it. Things can change on a dime if we first change our minds, change the way we have been thinking about our problems and our life. We don't have to wait. The Universe is always ready. We can release everything that we are finished with more quickly and easily. We just have to change our minds and keep them changed, keep them focused on the new experiences we want to enjoy.

The Power to do that is within every one of us. You have the power to decide on a new experience.

Can we stop complaining about what is and see a brighter, bigger, richer possibility right where we are? It's all there.

There is a powerful boil, or spring in Central Florida called Blue Springs. The water just keeps bubbling to the surface from the depths beneath. It can't help itself. That's what is happening in us. There is a great Power and Presence in you, an endless fountain of life and love just waiting for you to recognize and remember that you are that power right where you are. Remembering and knowing you have an intimate relationship with the very depths of who you are is the way you are guaranteed the life of your dreams, an extraordinary life.

Whatever is going on with those around you, as enticing and captivating as it might be, it's their life, and your life is yours. You have permission to keep yours going and to do all those things that keep you centered, loving and focused. You never have to put off your own life. There is a way to keep it in the middle of whatever is going on. In fact, it is essential that you do because that is what feeds and energizes you. There is something very great that wants to be experienced and it won't let you rest until it is, no matter what is happening around you. There is a way to do it all, to stay present and enjoy.

There is no guarantee that outside conditions will change the way we want them to in the world. The important thing is that *we* are forever changing, unfolding and becoming. We are forever expanding because of who we are. Even though our good may seem to come and go throughout our lives, we will keep on evolving. We will continue to feel richer, freer and more expansive within ourselves. No one can take that away from us. That is what we take with us when we leave this world. Your inner being is never affected by the things that go on in the physical world. We grow in our capacity to love and enjoy who we are along the way and most of all we grow in appreciation of this amazing relationship we have with Spirit. Our strength, our courage and our love increases as we keep on keeping on.

As I write my final words and collect the final things to say, I realize my whole life has been a journey to get me to this place where I am today. I had great help along the way, and could not have done any of it, without all of the support I have been given from Spirit operating in me, through me and all around me. From the mountaintop of my mind, I see magnificent beauty, the spectacular nature of Life. On my Sabbath, my day of rest, I look around and declare that it is all good and I know there is even more.

Some of the best advice I have ever received was to make my circle bigger. Now more than ever it is time to include more people in your own circle. Don't be afraid to ask for help. Seek out others who are like-minded and open to learning more about how Life really works and finding their special part in it. There is power in numbers. Find or create a group you feel close to and support it so that you can be a part of something larger than yourself and grow together. Then you will have even more to offer those around you and the world at large.

There may even be a Center for Spiritual Living in your area where you can practice living universal truth principles that apply to all people, everywhere. Such a Center will empower you and support you in being all you can be, and help you think the clearest, highest thoughts of truth you can grasp, because it is all about our thoughts and beliefs. They lead to how we feel. How we feel attracts to us great health and well-being, financial abundance and wealth, more loving and supportive relationships, more creative expression, or work and most of all, a closer, more intimate partnership with Spirit.

It is my sincere desire that what I have shared transcends any differences we may have of background, culture, religion, and nationality. I speak directly to the spirit of You. That's where we are One, living the One Life of Spirit together. We are more alike than we are different.

"Smooth Sailing" to you and remember, the words of the Master Teacher, Jesus, "Greater Works than these can you do also". And most of all, know that you are never alone.

I love you!

Cath

ADDENDUM

There are all kinds of Spiritual Practices. In Chapter 11, "Everything's a Practice", we discussed different tools and modalities to use as a starting place. Below are forms for the Ideal Day, Mind Treatment, Sacred Covenant and Sacred Space Covenant. Make copies for yourself. Once you have the form down, you can directly write it from memory in your own journal or vary it to suit you.

IDEAL DAY

Date: _____

My ideal day is filled with

_____

_____

_____

_____

_____

_____

I AM

_____

_____

_____

_____

_____

SPIRIT or Universe, I am ready to experience the following:

_____

_____

_____

_____

_____

_____

MAKE IT SO in a special way that only you can.

I follow my inner guidance and take the next action steps I know to take:

_____

_____

_____

_____

_____

_____

I AM grateful for:

_____

_____

_____

_____

_____

I AM grateful for highest and best happening for: (others)

_____

_____

_____

_____

I WHOLEHEARTEDLY ACCEPT ALL THIS and MORE. ...AND SO IT IS!

MIND TREATMENT

Topic or Desire: (what you want to do, have or be)

_____

_____

_____

_____

_____

Recognition (there's only one Creative Power, everywhere equally present)

_____

_____

_____

_____

Unification (I am embodying those same attributes)

_____

_____

_____

_____

Affirmation/Realization (that which I desire has already been given)

_____

_____

_____

*Denial (anything unlike what I desire has no power in itself or in my life)

_____

_____

_____

*Reaffirmation: (so I can have it)

_____

_____

_____

Gratitude (I am grateful to know it)

_____

_____

_____

Release (I don't have to know how to do it, I let go, let God figure out the how)

_____

_____

And so it is!

*optional

SACRED COVENANT

(Why am I here?)

I AM HERE TO:

_____

_____

_____

(I AM Statements or affirmations)

I AM:

_____

_____

_____

(Daily Agreements & Commitments)

I AGREE TO:

_____

_____

_____

THE UNIVERSE AGREES TO:

_____

_____

_____

_____

200

(Gratitude statement)

I AM GRATEFUL FOR:

_____

_____

_____

_____

_____

_____

(Dedications)

I DEDICATE MY LIFE TO:

_____

_____

_____

_____

_____

THE UNIVERSE DEDICATES IT'S LIFE TO:

_____

_____

_____

_____

(Closing) AND SO IT IS!

SACRED SPACE COVENANT

I live in a universe that welcomes me just as I am. IT, God, created me as a perfect expression of ITself. IT accepts me with unconditional love and provides me with the space I need to live comfortably and easily. I know this sacred space is essential to my well being. It frees me to accept my humanness, my imperfections and more and more appreciate my divine nature.

I freely and lovingly make this kind of space available to others who are near me, allowing them to be real and true, themselves. I extend my heart, I provide the wisdom available to me when asked, and choose words which neither impose nor judge but guide others in knowing what is right for them. I am divinely supported in knowing how to do this.

I give thanks for knowing sacred space is provided for us all. I enjoy living in a universe of love. And so it is!

Sacred Space Covenant:

I agree to listen and *be* present, not try to fix or give advice.

I agree to bring my best love and attention to whatever or whomever is before me, including and especially myself.

I agree to practice non-judgment.

I agree to love and accept myself and others as they are.

I agree to stay in the present, the *Now* moment of Power.

I use as my guide:

"If it is loving, if it grows, expands or deepens love, it's the right thing to do!"

Signed _____ Dated_____

My Favorite Movies

A Beautiful Mind

A Good Year

Brokeback Mountain

Castaway

Defending Your Life

Eat, Pray, Love

Elizabethtown

Feast of Love

Field of Dreams

Freedom Writers

Grand Canyon

Pay It Forward

Spirit

Star Trek – Next Generation series

The Great Debaters

Way of the Peaceful Warrior

My Favorite Books

Busting Loose from the Money Game – Robert Scheinfeld

Change Your Thinking Change Your Life – Wayne Dyer

Compass Points – Frank Henninger

Eat, Pray, Love – Elizabeth Gilbert

Edinburgh Lectures on Mental Science – Thomas Troward

Emerson's Essays – Ralph Waldo Emerson

Field of Dreams – Mary Manin Morrissey

Handbook to Higher Consciousness – Ken Keyes

How To Think Your Way to the Life You Want – Bruce Doyle III

Living in a Complaint Free World – Atwan Motwane

On Death and Dying – Elizabeth Kubler Ross

Power of Decision – Raymond Charles Barker

Practicing the Presence – Joel Goldsmith

Reflections on the Art of Living: A Joseph Campbell Companion – Diane K. Osbon

Science of Mind – Ernest Holmes

Science of Successful Living – Ernest Holmes

Spirit is Calling Journal – Chris Michaels, Edward Viljoen

Stones into Schools – Greg Mortenson

The Architecture of All Abundance – Lenedra Carroll

The Art of Allowing – Ester and Jerry Hicks

The Art of Deliberate Creation – Ester and Jerry Hicks

The Art of Racing in the Rain – Garth Stein

The Big Leap – Gay Hendricks

The Dynamic Laws of Prosperity – Catherine Ponder

The Millionaires of Genesis – Catherine Ponder

The Power of Now – Eckert Tolle

The Vortex – Ester and Jerry Hicks

This Thing Called You – Ernest Holmes

Three Cups of Tea – Greg Mortenson

Unveiling Your Hidden Powers – Emma Curtis Hopkins

You Can Heal Your Life – Louise Hay

Your Soul's Assignmet – Chris Michaels

Wise Women Don't Sing The Blues – Dr. Jane Claypool

Zero Limits – Joe Vitale and Dr. Hew Len

Acknowledgements

To my family, friends and colleagues, William John Zokan and Mary Crowley Zokan who taught me "Big Love" and gave me an example of living a religious/spiritual life. It was a framework from which I could begin. They continue to inspire me even though they are no longer here.

To my family and friends, for loving, accepting me and being there for me even when that was most difficult. I hold you in my heart always. To my three beautiful children, Nicholas, Elizabeth and Joseph, each so special in their own right. You couldn't ask for more beautiful beings to share your life. I am so grateful they picked me as their earth mother. They have been my greatest teachers, my best friends and they are a gift to the world by bringing a greater consciousness to all. Watch out world! To my ex-husband, Brad...I am forever grateful to him and his wife, Pam, for taking care of and raising our children when I could not. Thank you both for giving me the time I needed to put myself back together. To my ex-boyfriend, Steve, who was a bridge between worlds. He was with me during my darkest times and showed me how to survive in that place. He helped me to move into a whole, new life and for that I will always be grateful. To Molly, a guiding light who coached me and helped me purchase my very own condo. To my wonderful cousin, who helped save my life by introducing me to the beautiful teaching of Science of Mind and who continues to inspire, love and support me always. I am forever grateful. To Suzanne who has been a great support all these years. I will never forget sobbing over some guy in the back row of the church one Sunday and her searching for something in her purse to comfort me. She pulled out a beautiful topaz stone for me to hold. It brought me great comfort to see its beauty and feel its strength and most of all to sit between her and my cousin. To my younger, wonderful friend, Carol, who saw me through the "desert" time in my life, and is still always there for me. It's been an amazing journey together and she continues to be with me every step of the way. To Central Florida's Center for Spiritual Living, I appreciate having such a great community to work with these past 17 years and for the beautiful work we do together. You have supported me generously, making it possible for me to do what I love. I am forever grateful to my treatment partners and friends, Chris Michaels and Sam Goff, for our years together, for taking on the hard stuff of healing. To Sam, for our continued work on my deepest fears, pains, secrets and desires, and adding his rich perspective and love to my life. I am so blessed.

To Lousie Hay for your wonderful book, *You Can Heal Your Life* which we studied in Science of Mind class. I have continued to give away my book every time I got a new one and I continue to reference it as I work on myself and others. You are an inspiration to so many. Thank you. To Mary Manin Morrissey, my mentor and friend. I love, respect and honor who you are and your ability to keep on going in the midst of real life issues. Thank you for helping me through some tougher times as a minister. You are a beautiful example of what is possible.

I can't thank my first editor, Tara Treasurefield enough. She graciously held my hand through writing the main part of the book. It would never have been a book without her guidance. I am forever thankful to have her as my guide. To Barbara Hart, for being another editor and proofer. I can't thank you enough for cleaning things up and clarifying them. Endless hours! What a gift! To Matthew Aussprung, my nephew, who edited even more and proofed more. Countless hours and incredible dedication. You are a blessing! Thank you Joby, my wonderful sister-in-law, for your love and support and beautiful cover.

"Most of all a very special thanks to Michael Terranova and Wise Woman Press for believing in me and my project and transforming it into a book!"

About the Author

Cath DePalma is a pioneer in the study of higher consciousness and living a practical spirituality. She shares her life lessons, discoveries and experiences with others in a way that inspires and empowers them to move into a deeper, richer relationship with themselves, a more active, participatory relationship with the Universe, and a greater appreciation of the world around them. She has counseled, coached and inspired people for over 25 years. She co-directs the Central Florida Center for Spiritual Living with her husband, John. She has been a motivational speaker, teacher and writer for the past 18 years and has a unique gift for working with others as they move through transformation in their lives. She has three children, Nick, Liz and Joseph. Her new focus, "Journey Into Me", invites others to join her in a spiritual journey through classes, retreats and workshops. After her trip to Tanzania with International Outreach, she also helps coordinate Food Packaging Events at centers, churches, and organizations to feed the hungry in the U.S. and the world.

Where to purchase books and ebooks.

WiseWoman Press www.wisewomanpress.com

Amazon

DeVorss Publishing Co.

Cath DePalma: www.cathdepalma.org,

E-books through Barnes & Nobles,

 Kindle through Amazon,

Follow me on:

Facebook: www.facebook.com/cathdepalma2012

Twitter: www.twitter.com/cathdepalma2012

Website: www.cathdepalma.org

Available for speaking and workshops.

Cath DePalma at **cdepalma@ticl.org** or call C: (407)810-9044

Wise Woman Press

Vancouver, WA 98665
800.603.3005

Books Published by Wise Woman Press

Books by Emma Curtis Hopkins

- *Scientific Christian Mental Practice from the Original Booklets*
- *Resume*
- *The Gospel Series*
- *Class Lessons of 1888*
- *Self Treatments including Radiant I Am*
- *High Mysticism*
- *Genesis Series 1894*
- *Esoteric Philosophy in Spiritual Science*
- *Drops of Gold Journal*
- *Judgment Series*
- *Bible Interpretations: Series I, thru XXII*

By Ruth L. Miller

- *Unveiling Your Hidden Power: Emma Curtis Hopkins' Metaphysics for the 21st Century: Text, Workbook and Teachers Manual*
- *Coming into Freedom: Emily Cady's Lessons in Truth for the 21st Century*
- *The Power of Practice: Emily Cady Biography*
- *Power Beyond Magic: Ernest Holmes Biography*
- *Power to Heal: Emma Curtis Hopkins Biography*
- *The Power of Unity: Charles Fillmore Biography*
- *Power of Thought: Phineas P. Quimby Biography*
- *The Power of Insight: Thomas Troward Biography*
- *The Power of the Self: Ralph Waldo Emerson Biography*
- *Uncommon Prayer*
- *Spiritual Success*
- *Finding the Path*

Books Published by Wise Woman Press

By Malinda Cramer
- *Basic Statements and Health Treatment of Truth*
- *Lessons in the Science of Infinite Spirit and Christ method of Healing (Kindle and ebook only)*

By Ute Maria Cedilla
- *The Mysticism of Emma Curtis Hopkins Volume 1 Realizing the Christ Within*
- *The Mysticism of Emma Curtis Hopkins Volume 2 Ministry: Realizing The Christ One In All*

By Frances B. Lancaster
- *Abundance Now*
- *Happiness Now*
- *The 13th Commandment*
- *A Miracle of Love*

By Christine Green
- *Authentic Spirituality – A Woman's Guide to Living a Spiritually Empowered Life*
- *Anatomy of Caring*
- *A Caregivers Journal*

By Cath DePalma
- *I Can Do This Thing Called Life: and So Can You*

By Kathianne Lewis
- *40 Days to Freedom – with Emma Curtis Hopkins*
- *40 Days to Power – with excerpts of the work of Emma Curtis Hopkins*

By Joy Newell
- *Gracie's Adventures with God*

Most books are Available as ebooks and Kindle from Amazon and www.wisewomanpress.com